Hell Bound in My Sunday Best: WARdrobe Change Required

Carla DeBro

TRILOGY CHRISTIAN PUBLISHERS

TUSTIN, CA

Trilogy Christian Publishers
A Wholly Owned Subsidiary of Trinity Broadcasting Network
2442 Michelle Drive
Tustin, CA 92780

For information, address Trilogy Christian Publishing

Rights Department, 2442 Michelle Drive, Tustin, Ca 92780.

Trilogy Christian Publishing/ TBN and colophon are trademarks of Trinity Broadcasting Network.

For information about special discounts for bulk purchases, please contact Trilogy Christian Publishing.

Manufactured in the United States of America

10 9 8 7 6 5 4 3 2 1

Library of Congress Cataloging-in-Publication Data is available.
ISBN 978-1-64773-616-3
ISBN 978-1-64773-617-0 (ebook)

Contents

Dedication

This book could not have been written without my heavenly Father, who loved me enough to spare my life during my days of rebellion. I dedicate this book to Him for covering me despite my ungodly ways. With His love, I was able to persevere.

To my son Solomon, who always believes in the strength that is within me. His patience, support, and love for me is evident as he encourages me to believe in my abilities.

To my angelic son Donte', who watches over me and who has always been there for me, I would like to say thank you. I love and miss you very much.

To my sister Monica, thank you for all the free coaching sessions and advice that you gave me. From your strength, I grew courage. To my sister Laura, I love you for allowing me to grow to this place without condemnation. You are my big sister who sees more in me than I often neglect to see. Lastly, to my good friends

Patricia and Phyllis, I would like to thank you for being a beacon of hope when I felt broken.

Foreword

If you've ever dealt with unforgiveness, an identity crisis, defeating thoughts, or living in total opposition of God's purpose, this book is for you. Many people dress up in their Sunday's best on any given day of the week to put forth a good front but are often wearing a mask to pretend and are hiding behind painful wounds.

After reading *Hellbound in My Sunday's Best: WARdrobe Change Required*, readers will receive reinforcement on the importance of transforming their minds through the Word of God and by spending time with Him. Carla eloquently shares transparent and intimate moments from her past, such as how she released herself to God and yielded to His correction and healing. She reminds us that when we change, we shouldn't allow others to pull us back to the past cycle of destruction.

The authentic transparency that flows throughout this book will allow some readers to empathize and others to sympathize with the strongholds presented in its writings. Listening to the Holy Spirit can transform our lives. This book will open your eyes to the tactics that Satan uses to attempt to throw God's children off course and make them journey down a path of self-destruction.

Action items are insightfully given for when we need to adjust our thoughts and our responses to situations so God can reign in our lives. They also allow God to change us internally to see ourselves as He does. The biblical insights and references allow readers to further engage with the Word of God. The importance of listening to the Holy Spirit, repenting, and asking for forgiveness is a common message for us to remember. There are clear reminders in this book of the importance of forgiving ourselves, others, and embracing that God forgives us. As Carla writes, "When you ask for forgiveness, smile, because you are making progress towards being obedient to our Lord."

—Dr. Monica DeBro,
author, speaker, mentor, and advocate against
domestic violence

Acknowledgements

It was so exciting to see how God allowed the words to flow from my spirit to written text. He placed people in my life who provided support throughout the process, and with their presence, I know I had a winning team who wanted me to succeed.

It is with great love and admiration that I must thank my sister Monica for her presence throughout the various stages of this book. She shared her insight and provided guidance so that I could complete each chapter knowing that if things changed, it was okay, because God works like that. I love you, sis!

Even though my son Solomon felt that I was always busy, he was patient and very understanding. I want to thank him for always encouraging me to believe in my dreams and to keep moving forward so that I could complete this book. You are my best son on earth, and I love you.

To my big sister Laura, you are truly amazing. Thank you for your encouragement to keep taking steps to make my life as God had shown me it should be. You have always taken care of us since we were children and you still do. Much love to you forever.

For the love and support from Gwendolyn, David, and Ovell, I want to say thank you. You guys are phenomenal, and you always provided input that helped me know that I am loved and that I can do all things through Christ. I will forever love and treasure your presence in my life.

Learning to love beyond limits is what my mother and father Rev. and Mrs. W. L. DeBro taught me . It was their love for me which drew me closer to God. They instilled the foundation for loving Christ. It was this foundation that prepared me so I could be receptive when the Holy Spirit opened my eyes to who God is and how He lovingly reveals His word for my growth in Him. For this reason, I am extremely grateful to have parents who showed me faith in God.

I want to give a special "thank you" to Mark and the Trinity Publishing team for believing in the message God gave me to share. Your willingness to commit to publishing this book encouraged me to complete each thought. I look forward to working with you on many more endeavors, and I am forever grateful for your support.

Finally, to all those who took from me and brought me closer to my broken place, I want to thank you, because what you meant to be evil, God allowed to happen, and He turned it into a marvelous transformation. I have been delivered from my brokenness and made whole and complete in my Father.

Preface

As you read this book, you will notice that I do not tell you exactly what the scriptures say. I did this so that you can find them and read them for yourself. I would like to encourage you to get a Bible. I know that many of us use a Bible app, but there is so much in the Word that you need to see for yourself. With your own physical Bible, you get to see the written text from God. You are not relying on an app – instead, a physical Bible connects you to the Word. It is a book. It is a book written by men who were directed by God. Who knows what the future holds for these apps? Slowly, words in the Bible might begin to change. You might not be able to question the text because you would not have the written word to challenge it, so I encourage you to please get your own physical Bible. Use it daily and walk with God. According to Revelation 21:8, all other paths lead to the second death.

There are sections in this book where I was reluctant to tell the full truth, but the Holy Spirit reminded me that God had freed me from my past, so there is nothing anyone can say to put me in bondage, not even you, so as you read this book, know that I told it all so that you would not have anything to gossip about. I am free, and now I want to free others through my struggles and faith in God.

When you become free, do not worry about the feeling of loneliness, because God will fill you with His presence. He will provide you with someone you can talk to. I have two people that I share with, and I trust them to tell me the truth at all times. I suggest that you identify those people in your life who will not put up with your foolishness. They will keep you in check and remind you of what God says. Their suggestions will equip you for this journey, so take heed to them, as they are going to confirm what God is telling you. I am so excited to share my life's journey – from my fall from grace to my acceptance into redemption.

I am no longer afraid (see Isaiah 54:17). You shouldn't be, either.

Introduction

Getting up early on Sunday (one of the few days that you have off from work), finding your outfit that says, "I've got it together", and putting on your sparkling heels that help make your outfit complete is a part of your weekend routine. You do all of this so you can go to church, even though the preparation and the action of going does not make you feel whole like you believe you should feel. However, you do it because it is expected of you. You go because your parents went. You smile at everyone because you do not want them to know the truth: that you spent last night struggling with your perceived reality as you guzzled down two bottles of wine. You go to church in hopes of finding something that will fill the void that plagues your life. However, after each church service, you go home, and you still feel as if there is something missing.

With this in mind, you begin to listen to others who share their love stories and great times. You wonder what is really the matter with you, and you start to ask God what you have done to deserve this feeling of emptiness. At some point, you start comparing yourself with others – you start to think that everyone has it together except you and that there is no hope for you. These are all *lies*. Shut the door on them and run to the next chapter of your life. If you must, leave your sparkling heels behind and get going.

Run to the place where you can find the truth in knowing that you are worth saving. God cares for you. Find hope in learning who He says you are, because I am here to tell you that there is hope for you. You can never go too far from God. He will chase after you because He loves you. Listen, if Jesus went to Hades to save those who were lost, trust me – He cares about you too. He wants to save you because He loves you. He has a purpose for your life. You just need to make the decision to make a WARdrobe change, too, and put on the armor of God. He rescued me from a life of lies, deception, sex, and marijuana. Believe me when I tell you that I only survived because He cared for me. You will survive too. Just implement God's plan for your life. A plan that starts with forgiveness.

CHAPTER 1

Struggling Believer

As a child, I was dragged to church every Sunday morning from 8:45 a.m. until around 2:00 p.m. Getting out at 2:00 p.m. was early, because if the church had a program, that meant I was going to be there much later. Sometimes, I was stuck at church until well after five o'clock in the evening. If the doors of the church were open, I was there – church clean up, special programs, church meetings, and revival. It did not matter what the cause was; I was a mandated attendant. One time, I even missed the airing of the *Dallas* episode, "Who Shot J.R.". I remember missing this episode because when we went to revival that night, my father—who was our preacher—cleverly used this as the title of his sermon topic. Only my father could think to have this as the topic of his sermon, and to this day he still makes me smile with his cleverness.

While at church, I spent countless hours wishing I could be like the children who lived across the street. They got to play outside all day on Sunday, and they never regularly went to any church. I would always see them having a good time as I peered outside the church window. Perhaps that is why my father later put stained glass contact paper on the windows. While there were many times when I had fun at church, it was years later in life that I realized that even though I did not like being in church all the time, it was far better than playing with friends. I did not appreciate the value of my church-rearing back then, but I sure do value it now, unlike those children, who I thought were the lucky ones.

I still recall the day I accepted Christ into my life. I was at St. Paul Missionary Baptist Church in the small town of Helena, Arkansas, where I grew up. Prior to church starting that night, I was outside in my church dress, jumping ditches and enjoying life like many eight-year-old children my age did. When service began that evening, I sat there in the front pew in church, and as the invitation to accept Jesus into my life was offered, I agreed to join the church and be a Christian. If I am honest, I do not know if I did it because I was expected to join or if it was because God was calling me to join. I do know that my parents never pressured me to join the church, but somehow, I just knew it was the right thing to do. On the day I said "yes" to Jesus, I am sure my parents' hearts leapt for joy. I am positive that they were always concerned about me because of my ability to find alternative ways to do things instead of following instructions. I am so glad they only knew part of what I did, which meant I really didn't get all the whippings I deserved. I can tell you that the ones I *did* get made up for the ones I didn't get.

Anyway, I did not really know what I was getting myself into as a new Christian. There wasn't a class to inform me about what I should do next, so you know that there was also no class to teach me what I should not do. This meant that I was left to figure it out on my own. Oh boy, did that take a while. Because I was clueless and did not study the Bible for my own understanding, I was vulnerable to what others said I could and couldn't do. Although I grew up in church and heard my father minister to me about Jesus, I did not know to look in the Bible to find what I needed for this journey. Perhaps I loved how my father vividly told the stories in the Bible, so I felt his word was enough to bring the Bible to life. As I reflect, I realize that most sermons were about people being baptized by John and Jesus being tortured by the king's soldiers. Most other sermons were about not breaking the Ten Commandments and how you would go to hell for breaking them. You see, my father was a "fire and brimstone" type of minister who was loving and caring. In listening to his sermons, I didn't recall much about what to do if you did break a commandment. Yes, I knew that I had to pray and ask for forgiveness, but how long was God going to stay mad at me? Yes, I knew that God forgave me, but why did I feel so guilty? How was I supposed to pray? Would God kick me out of His kingdom for breaking the commandments? These unanswered questions left me feeling very confused and isolated.

Another issue I had was understanding how the Bible related to my life. As a child, I struggled to connect to the stories in the Bible because I thought they were just like the nonfictional stories in other books I read. I did not know how to apply them to my life, so I had many questions. Some of these are questions that many believers still have, and they should be answered by us.

Hopefully, as you read this book, you will realize the grace of God and how much He really loves us – not as the world loves us, but unconditionally and not based on anything but who we really are. God is waiting on us to come to Him so He can teach us how to walk in His love and help save others. That is why it was so important for Paul to be saved. He was saved to give people like us hope. He was saved to show us that God loved him even when he was going around bad-mouthing Christians and voting for them to be put to death.

Paul's life is an example of the extent our Father will go to save us, because His desire is for us to forever be with Him. That is real love.

As a child, after being saved by saying, "I believe in Jesus" (and yes, that is it; that is all we have to do; mind you, you do need to actually believe), I recall an older sibling of my friend telling me that since I joined church and was a Christian, I could not jump rope. I remember thinking, *Really?!* Meanwhile, it never occurred to me that even though she was a Christian, too, she was also jumping rope. So, I did not jump rope for a while—at least not that day. I thought her words were true, because I knew my dad did not let me ride my bike on Sundays, and at that point I was thinking, *I can't even jump rope ever again! What is this Christian thing that I just joined? How in the world am I supposed to live the rest of my life not jumping rope?* To make matters worse, she told me that something bad would happen to me if I jumped rope! I was so scared to jump rope, and because I did not want to get in trouble when I secretly jumped rope, I never talked to my dad about it. Of course, weeks later, I realized she was lying.

That is the danger of not informing Christians on how to apply God's Word to their lives. Explaining the Bible on a level that is understandable to people with various relationships with God can reduce misunderstandings. When new believers accept God as their Father, it is vital that they are provided with support so that they can learn what God truly says. Not preparing young saints for this spiritual battle leaves them vulnerable to become victims of Satan. Informing them how their lives will be impacted due to the enemies having marked them as one who is aspiring to trust in God helps them understand why challenges come and how they should respond.

Leaving our Christian sisters and brothers to fight the battle alone is like watching someone sinking in quicksand. You and I both know that we do not have a chance when we fight these battles by ourselves. Without being aware of our gift from God, which is the Holy Spirit, our lives are in constant turmoil. Without the powerful spiritual warfare God activated in our lives, the world of principalities would defeat us. There have been many times where the spirits of darkness began to stalk me so that they could prevent me from knowing how much my Father loves me. I have gotten better at fighting off the malicious thoughts that they put in my head by reminding myself that my heavenly Father loves me. His love for us was so grand that He gave us the Holy Spirit so that we can deflect Satan's attacks.

As believers, when we do not understand the power of the Holy Spirit, the battle is a great struggle, as the demons have an unfair advantage. It can appear as if these spirits know more about the believer than the believer knows about themselves. Providing support for each other helps us win because the God in us is greater than any spiritual force of evil that attacks. If God is for us, who can be against us? Absolutely no one.

CHAPTER 2

Help Wanted: Dressmaker Needed

We must remember that these spirits of darkness know the scriptures and they try to use their insight to destroy us. They are following Satan and have been in heaven, so they understand how powerful our Father is. They know their mission, which is to get us to doubt God. They come together for a common purpose and work collectively to keep us from walking in faith, yet we do not work collaboratively as we should to help each other. Instead, we tend to allow Christian friends to proceed through life by giving them a Bible and wishing them good luck. Heck, if I am honest, we often do not even give them a Bible at all nowadays. We might tell them about the Bible app, but I personally think we need a physical Bible because it is tangible and will remind us to read it by physically being present in our space. I have also learned that when I am reading a scripture from a physical Bible, I often end up reading more scriptures than I would have if I had used the app.

Let me go back and clarify what I said earlier regarding the spirits of darkness knowing the scriptures. When I said this, I meant they can recite them, but they do not understand them (see Matthew 13:11-15). The Bible was written so that believers could know about their Father and His kingdom with the guidance of the Holy Spirit. The Bible is living and active, so each time you read it, you might get a different message from God (see Hebrews 4:12). That is why Satan wants to distract us from reading the Word. The scriptures were written to give us encouragement and hope (see Romans 15:4). As Christians, it is our responsibility to help and encourage each other to live by faith instead of gossiping about one another and discouraging each other. These reactions do not plant good seeds; instead, they lead to the seed of God being destroyed or damaged. When we decide to walk with Christ (and I mean *really* walk with Him by allowing the Holy Spirit to guide, protect, and direct us), the Holy Spirit will speak to us and remind us every time we go astray. This reminder also comes when gossip hits our ear. The Holy Spirit will say immediately, "That is gossip. Do not participate!" In case you are wondering how I know, it is because He speaks to me in this manner. Sometimes, I will engage in the conversation and say what I am burning to say on that topic because I just want to participate. After saying a sentence or two, the Holy Spirit will say, "I told you not to discuss this issue." So, immediately, I ask for forgiveness and I disengage. Disengaging may sometimes mean to stop talking to the person and getting off the phone, or it might mean changing the subject. Either way, the common practice of gossiping should not be a part of our Christian lives. It is not like we are listening or participating so that we can offer help. Let's be honest – we love a good tidbit of gossip. If this was not true, then there would be no need for magazines that support such gossiping behavior. Gossiping is a hindrance. Alteration in our attitude is needed so that we can help others in their pain in order for them to feel encouraged instead of overwhelmed by the enemy. Cease gossiping and start warning, helping, and encouraging.

The danger of not informing our sisters and brothers about the tricks of the enemy leads to them being unprepared for the daily tests that they will encounter. This lack of test preparation is like when someone must prepare for an anatomy test on bones. They are allowed to spend quality time studying, and their preparation makes them feel as if they are ready for the test because they know all 206 bones, their function, and location. However, when the teacher hands out the test, it's full of chemistry formulas that the student did not think to study about.

In life, we have tests that we seem to fail. Test failure happens because we are either misinformed about the test topic or not fully informed about what the test would cover. The results would be the same: a low grade along with feelings of failure, which can lead to feelings of inadequacy. This test analogy is how many of us have felt when we do not perform in the way Christ would expect us. To prevent having feelings of failure and to avoid certain events having a traumatic effect on our walk with Christ, we (yes, we) need to save each other. If we do not, then feelings of inadequacy will begin to seep into our daily thoughts. This predicament is all Satan needs to start putting untruths into our heads.

It is time-out for allowing Satan to intervene in our lives as if he has authority. Our job is to hold each other accountable by not encouraging each other to participate in sin and by helping one another when we do sin. It is time to save each other by showing love and compassion, because along this journey, we need each other as a support group. We are the best support organization in the world as long as we support one another by allowing the Holy Spirit to minister to us. Our support system is so powerful that the prayers of one believer can defeat a thousand unwanted spirits because the Lord fights for us (see Joshua 23:10). He is in the midst of our prayers, causing things to happen in our favor (see Matthew 18:20).

When we do not operate collaboratively, it leaves us feeling helpless and lonely on this journey. Our lack of support for each other allows Satan to wreak havoc in the lives of believers as he constantly sends messages that remind us of our shortcomings. It is like he is using a megaphone to make sure we hear him when he tells us our inabilities and our failures. When we receive what Satan says, we allow him to cause us to live with limited possibilities, when in reality, our Father can do more than we can think or imagine in our lives (see Ephesians 3:20). Satan needs a daily eviction notice so we can live in victory. That is what our Father wants for us: a victorious life.

In the beginning, my misunderstanding about Christianity caused me to be unable to comprehend how God expected me to function with all of these limitations. I did not understand how God could be so loving yet prevent a child from enjoying the simple things in life like riding a bike on Sunday and jumping rope. I also remembered another reason why I did not tell my father about the jump rope incident. I assumed it was a rule he did not know, so I was not going to tell him because I loved jumping rope. I thought that if he caught me jumping rope, I would be okay. Because of man's rules, I did not know God as my caring Father, so I really did not see Him as loving to children, and I had heard sermons referencing how Jesus said, "Suffer little children who come unto me." With this thought in mind, I thought I was destined to suffer because I was a child who was coming to Jesus. I loved jumping rope and riding my bike, and I sure didn't understand how He got pleasure out of my suffering. I guess I really should have asked clarifying questions.

Because I did not receive godly insight on a level I could understand, I felt like Christians were not allowed to have fun! I am sure this is how some believers feel too as there are many rules in the Mosaic law that left believers feeling unworthy because of all the stipulations. They do not understand that we are no longer under these laws. Even though I know that we have a new covenant because of Jesus, I always thought Christians did not have fun or fun gatherings – at least that was how things were when I was a child. I felt like the only time they would get together was to hear sermons that reminded them of how good others are. Sometimes, these types of sermons can leave us feeling inadequate.

Let me clear up the feelings of inadequacy before we go any further. First, God never says we are inadequate. As believers and as heirs of the kingdom, we will make mistakes, but we should not ridicule ourselves with negative thoughts. We just need to identify what we did wrong, ask God to forgive us, and stop doing it. Sure, you might commit the same sin several times and you might not even ask for forgiveness for years, but when you do, God will forgive you immediately. Once you ask for forgiveness, continue to encourage others to make changes, too.

When you do decide to change, please know that others will not like it. You will lose friends, but that is okay. Do not get angry with them, but instead accept that they were in your life for a season. Keep them in prayer and ask your Father what He needs you to do. Also, when you say you are changing, you will be presented with many opportunities to go back to that life. Just be prepared to say, "No." Do not try to justify how you have changed and how you will not fall all the way back into that sin. See this invitation to step back into your bad habit as an opportunity to embrace what you know is wrong. Do not compromise. Pray and leave it alone, because your Father has a better plan for your life.

Some churches have gotten better at providing children with valid information about who Jesus is. They have a children's church service to help children realize that being a Christian really does not mean they will suffer. Also, when people join church, there are often meetings to tell new members about the rules of the church, as I have attended several "new members" classes during my walk with Christ. Perhaps having a class on how to overcome would be more practical and realistic. I recall attending a new members class in which the pastor, Elder Boden, spoke of his marijuana use and how he had changed his life. I love Elder Boden for telling the truth about his past. He was real. He told the truth about his struggle, and he was not ashamed of his past. He allowed others to see that even though your past may be a little shady, it is okay, because God still loves us. He was one of the few church leaders who I thought told the real truth so others could be inspired.

I wish more Christian leaders would be this honest. I am sure it would save so many more non-believers and it would help believers too. However, when Christians get saved, there is a tendency to forget how God had mercy on us. We tend to think we are better than anyone else, so we leave others who have the same challenge lost in a maze. Go somewhere and sit yourself down! Ask the Holy Spirit to minister to you so that you can see your faults. I promise that you have them. You just need to see them; stop with your mouth of negativity and help others who have similar struggles.

I know some of you like to say, "I love everyone." My questions to you are: do you love like Jesus does? Do you see division; meaning do you think that homosexuals are not loved by God? Do you think that murderers do not have the right to be saved? God would call you a hypocrite. First of all, we all sin, and if I am honest with you, I used to think that my sin was not as bad as others even though I was aware of how God viewed sin (see Romans 3:9). It is time for fake religious practices to end so that we can minister to each other. Our ways have led many non-believers to run away from the church because we represent ourselves and not our Father! Our fake ways negatively impact new believers and non-believers. We are dressed up like Christians, but we are playing for the other side.

Our ways allow spiritual principalities of darkness to teach their rules of the game of life. This practice is designed to keep Christians from being in the championship game. Why? We do not protect each other. It is our job to hold each other's hand and say that it is okay (see Genesis 4:9). I have had to take this test in life several times before I understood what God was teaching me. However, when we shrug our shoulders at each other and act as if we are indifferent because their lifestyle choices are not ours, we are not being examples as Christ would have us.

Let's look at one of my favorite people in the Bible – Paul. I love him because if God can love this man, then surely He can love me. You see, I am being judgmental in thinking my life is better than Paul's, but I want you to know that we persecute Christians daily through our actions. Anyway, let me continue with why I love Paul, because his presence radiates love. Paul persecuted so many Christians. Wait – let me step back so that you can understand *how* he persecuted Christians. Paul did *not* like Christians. I would go so far as to say he *hated* Christians. I say this because he traveled around to many different places to identify anyone who confessed that they were believers. I am sure he did not just knock on their doors and say for them to come with him. I am sure he saw those helping him gather Christians mistreat the Christians, and he probably threw a punch or two as he walked them around, taking them to be judged as violators of the law. Let's be clear – the Bible does not say that he was the one who killed the Christians, but he did participate in ending their lives.

That is how we behave. You see, we don't have to be the one who inflicts physical wounds, but our actions do more harm than we would like to admit. Our words cause those who are in the world to struggle even more because we do not want to tell our truth. We also cause many believers to be in the sandpit for way too long. Let me share with you how we do this. We want to keep a secret about the truth; about how we were abused or how sinful our lives were. Even though we go to church every Sunday, our presence does not convey our struggle with lust or our struggle with drug addiction, so we remain silent.

Get over yourself and help someone else with your truth. It is time for God's army to rise up, and when we rise with compassion for everyone, it will positively impact the world. Trust me—no, better yet, trust God. If you help one person, that is good Christian work (see Luke 15:1-7). If the angels rejoice every time someone confesses to Jesus, don't you want to be connected to that celebration in Heaven? Save one person that would have remained lost, damaged, or hurt by reaching out to them. If you remain silent, you will save no one.

Now, we will get back the beginning of my walk with Christ as a new Christian. Well, the misinformation about jumping rope made my walk with Christ a struggle from the beginning, because as a child, remember that the church did not tell me how I could apply the Bible to my life. Although I loved the stories my father told during his sermons, I did not know about the real areas in which I should be knowledgeable as a Christian. There were no classes about sex in a way that I could understand as a child. There was sex education in public school, but the messages they taught were different. Yes, the church used those big words like "fornication" and "adultery", but I did not have a clue what those words meant. For this reason, I believe it is important to have a children's church service no matter how small or large your congregation is—no, not to talk about sex, but to tell them how forgiving and loving God is.

Children need to be given an opportunity to understand and relate the Word to their lives. If they are not given this chance, then the Bible is just a book of stories about a powerful God. Children need biblical instruction on a level they can understand. When they are sitting in the church and do not know half of what the pastor is saying, it leads to misinformation or lack of knowledge. This is one time in which misinformation and lack of knowledge is extremely dangerous (see Hosea 4:6). It does not matter how good the preacher "hoops", children will still be lost and confused. Some of you may not know what "hooping" is, but many ministers implement this technique in the South. As a matter of a fact, if a minister couldn't "hoop", people would say he couldn't preach. If you still do not know what "hooping" is, Google it. I am sure you will find several videos.

That form of ministering has its place, but God's children need to be taught the truth about how much God loves them. Understanding God's love and compassion for us helps us with our faith walk. For this reason, it is important to share how God has shown His love to us. Like I said, children need to be taught about God on a level they can understand. As I was rereading this text, the Holy Spirit said that it is not just children who are identified by their biological age, but all of God's children who come to learn of His ways that need teaching on a level they can understand. This includes you and

I, because if we are not living the life God promised us, then we need to gain a better understanding of how to walk in faith.

Greater understanding is needed regarding concepts like how to pray, the importance of reading the Bible, and the truth about who we are. These topics are important because the world has told us who we are for so long, and because we listened to the world, we have tried to fit in. That is why sharing with others that they have the Holy Spirit in them is so powerful. It helps us understand that we are not alone in our Christian journey. Understanding these concepts will help us develop a relationship with God. His daily presence in our lives will become more evident as we connect to Him. When learning about God, it is important to understand that we do not take a first grader and put them in college, expecting them to keep up with the class. That practice is insane. So, why do we expect children or new believers to understand the mysteries of God and to totally understand the Word of God when they are put in the sanctuary with everyone else? I am not knocking the power of the Holy Spirit and His ability to speak with anyone, but I *am* emphasizing that many of us have questions that need answering. Therefore, providing a platform for an opportunity to have this conversation would be extremely helpful.

Opportunities to gain an explicit understanding of our God on various platforms can provide instruction that increases the faith of all believers. Okay, maybe you have Sunday school at your church and you think that is sufficient. However, if we are honest, how many people attend Sunday school? How many churches still *teach* Sunday school? If we really break it down and look at the churches that teach Sunday school, we have to look at the books that are used for instruction. Many of those lessons were a challenge for me to connect to, and I am sure others feel the same way. I often felt that when people read those scriptures, they used them to talk about the mistakes that *others* made, not *my* mistakes. Those books did not speak about my life, nor did the teacher connect those scriptures to my world. The scriptures spoke about people in a time period that did not reflect the things I saw daily. A common thought that I had was, *Those people sure do fight a lot.*

CHAPTER 3

Alterations Required

I recall teaching the Good News Club at the elementary school where I was working as a teacher. The Good News Club shared the Bible with children after school. Let me be clear – I could have been a better Good News Club teacher, even though every Thursday I was there to present the lesson to the children. Why was I not the best? Well, most of the time, I prepared the lesson during my lunch break, during my students' recess break, or throughout the day on the day that I was going to present the lesson. I did not spend as many hours preparing at home as I should have, nor did I do much praying about how to present the lesson. Yes, I did prepare some at home, but many times, I was at work completing the finishing touches.

Don't get me wrong – it was great to share the Word with the children. I felt so happy to see their smiling faces. As a matter of a fact, our school had more children who attended the Good News Club than any other school in our district. Many days, there were more than one hundred children who came to learn about Jesus. They had questions, and parents volunteered to help. I recall one family in which the mother would come early to pick up one sibling when school was dismissed, but she would come back to pick up the other sibling because he wanted to learn about Jesus in the Good News Club. I am bringing this up because I want you to see that there is a great need for our children to learn about Jesus, and it is our responsibility to help them. Children want to learn about who Jesus is, and as Christians, supporting the Good News Club or any Christian-based organization that goes into public education to share the Word of God is a good program to support. There are many ways you can support, including volunteering, making financial contributions, or donating refreshments.

Let me stop now and ask God to forgive me for my ways. Now, I am forgiven, so let me continue with this point. Yes, I was not the best teacher, because I did not prepare in advance, and on one occasion, as I was instructing the children, I answered the phone and told the person that I would have to call him back because I was teaching. Yes, along this journey you will make mistakes, even when you are in the midst of doing something good for Christ, but these are opportunities for growth. Stop gasping and saying that you would never do something like that. I am talking about these honest incidents so that we can help each other. Our life struggles will help others to know that God is forgiving, and when we share God's love, we need to speak from a heart of love, not one of condemnation. During this journey, we will make mistakes, but just as soon as we recognize our wrongdoing, asking for forgiveness grants us permission to continue to know that we are forgiven. Yes, just as soon as you ask for forgiveness, you are forgiven (see 1 John 1:9). Some of your sins or mistakes might seem like they are colossal, but they are not. God sees all sin the same, and these sins are learning steps in the journey to be like Christ. Besides, when God sees a believer, He does not see them as sinners, but as His righteous children (see 2 Corinthians 5:21).

When teaching others, it is important to be mindful of actions. Dressing up on Halloween was one of my favorite activities. Even though my other Christian coworker did not participate in it, I didn't see anything wrong with it until I remembered that one of my Christian sisters had gently told me that this was not good to do. I reflected on her kind words and stopped. During instruction, I shared with the children that I was not going to participate anymore because I received the corrections from my sister in Christ advising me to stop participating in the holiday. When I made this

announcement, my friend said, "I didn't tell you that."
I was so puzzled because I distinctly recalled having
that conversation with her. Apparently, it happened in
a dream, but the memory was so strong that I actually
believed it transpired in real life. God used the right
person in my dream to warn me, because had it been
anyone else, I probably would not have listened to them.

The bad thing about working in our own strength is
that exhaustion can cause us to be impatient. I am sure
there were times when I was impatient and exhausted,
which caused some children not to come back. One of
those children was a girl named Stephanie. Stephanie
is a very intelligent young lady who I had taught in the
second grade. She was a helpful leader with a great
demeanor. Because of my impatience, she stopped attending Good News Club. My behavior impacted her
decision to disengage in learning about Jesus. When
our behavior negatively impacts others, pray for change
not just for ourselves, but also for their lives, too. For
this reason, I have to pray for Stephanie from this day
forward, as I saw a spirit beginning to infuse her life
shortly after she stopped coming to the Good News
Club. Now, do not think that I did not see Stephanie
and ignored her. She is a good person, and I care about
her wellbeing. I just had not gained the understanding
that I have now, and if I did, I would have compelled her
to come back with a little more persuasion of compas-

sion. I believe in my heart that she is not lost and is a believer who God is watching over.

Volunteering as a Good News Club instructor had many benefits, as I worked with other believers at the school. Each of us had our jobs to do when providing the lessons for the students, and there were days where I know we all felt exhausted from our instructional day, but we worked together to help the children learn more about Jesus. Not only did we provide instruction, games, songs, and prayer, but we provided all the snacks, and when the drinks went on sale, we made sure we collected an abundance so that we would have enough for the semester. We knew that children wanted to know about Jesus, and it would be selfish of us not to provide snacks, because they had been at school all day and some of them were not going to go home until six o'clock in the evening. I mention this because often, we only see the surface of how things are, but God wants us to think towards the nature of what people need so that we can serve them without their minds being distracted.

It was very gratifying for me to see so many children who were curious about Jesus. We had real talks about the Bible and I enjoyed their questions. Of course, none of them asked me if jumping rope as a Christian was wrong. Their questions were more out of curiosity, but curiosity is the beginning of a seed that plants and grows. Planting seeds is what Jesus did, and likewise, we should too. This seed led to the children being excited about Jesus. The children were so excited to participate that we had a list of them who wanted to lead the class in prayer. I get just as much satisfaction today as I reflect on those days as I did when we taught the lessons. It was an awesome experience, as they were honestly seeking to know about our Father.

This wasn't my first time teaching children about God. I have taught them during Sunday church service. Continuous service to the children became challenging after a season or two because I never went inside church to enjoy the message, and I often felt that I missed out. I am sure you are thinking, *Why she is telling me this?* I would like to strongly encourage you to volunteer at your church to teach children. Many times, people will avoid the children's ministry like it is a plague. They don't want to have anything to do with the children, but these little ones need us! Volunteering once a month can make a big difference in their lives. Children need opportunities to have their small group learning instruction. As they engage in the lessons, they become more aware of who God is and what He thinks about them. Helping children learn about God is vital to bringing the mysteries of God to them in a way that they can apply it to their lives. Another opportunity to share God with children is by volunteering to help at a school program. This will allow you to minister to someone and will hopefully get you to look at your Bible before Sunday during service. Yes, I know it happens, because I am guilty of this style of Christian living too.

Reading the Bible is a requirement when sharing the Word. Here is a list of reasons why we might not spend time reading the Bible:

1. We are too busy.
2. We have other responsibilities.
3. We do not have a Bible.
4. We fall asleep every time we open the Bible.
5. We are not dealing with a crisis in which we feel that we need God.
6. We believe we can solve the problem on our own.
7. We are in a crisis and we do not have time.
8. Whatever your reason is, list it here; I am sure it is not a good enough excuse for you to neglect an opportunity to connect with our loving Father:

_____

Yes, all those excuses are really good if you do not want to know why the world is designed to keep us from learning the truth that is written in God's Word. I have never been someone who did not want to learn. I really find being knowledgeable exciting because it allows me to engage in conversations with so many. However, I did not read my Bible for many of the reasons listed above. The Holy Spirit has brought me to the place where I set the goal to read my Bible and pray daily. I am not referring to the bedtime prayer or the quick, "Thank You, Jesus for waking me up this morning," prayer. I spend time praying while doing daily activities, like when I walk my dogs. Why was this time chosen for me? Every day, I walk my dogs, so walking the dogs for me equates to spending time in prayer. Notice that I said why was this time chosen for me. I did not choose this time, but God did. Having a routine in our life that is focused around God allows an opportunity for us to hear from God. Yes, there are days where I think, *Ugh, I don't want to walk today.* I will say that I do not want to walk because I am tired, or I will say I am only walking one mile. While walking my dogs, I don't answer my phone unless it is my son, and I make sure that I spend this time focused on God. Of course, there are moments when I find my mind wandering and I have to refocus my thoughts. The important thing is that making time for our Father is significant. It helps us to deal with all our emotional challenges and it gives us wisdom throughout the day. Finding time to spend with God is helpful in directing you to share the Bible with others, especially children.

Hopefully, you are now willing to volunteer to work with children in your church. Here are some other opportunities to offer your assistance: if your church has a summer church for the children, or if your church has vacation Bible school, volunteer to work with them. I know you may be thinking, *That is not my gift. I do not want to work with children.* Why? Evaluate why this is, and unless you are a child molester or have thoughts of molesting children, I would suggest that you volunteer.

These children are vulnerable to the evil things that lay ahead, and you know how to help them because the Holy Spirit will guide you if you ask Him. Your presence in a child's life could help them see how valuable they are. Your insight could save a child who needs encouragement. I believe that if you have experienced any form of hurt, your hurt can be used to help others. Our children need us to speak into their lives to help them see their value and to know that they are loved. Be the one to help children see that Christianity is not what the world says. Help them find their value through your caring heart. Your presence will make a difference.

CHAPTER 4

Ironing Out the Ruffles

As we peek into the reality of who I was, I would like to express the truth about the power of the spirit of seduction and how loneliness combined with seduction leads to disobedience. Seduction and loneliness connect us to the selfishness that dwells in us and illuminates when we are out to satisfy our desires. When we seek to fulfill our flesh without considering the consequences, our sacrifice leads us down a dangerous path. However, if you are like me, when we decide that we want something, we will obtain what we want regardless of the conflict it creates within.

There are times when we are most vulnerable to the spirit of loneliness. For some of us, loneliness creeps up on us during certain seasons of our lives. When vulnerability causes us to embrace loneliness, we make choices that we would not usually make. We accept things from men that we would not usually accept, even though we know that acting in this manner conflicts with God. Our minds are challenged to follow the warnings from the Holy Spirit. Slowly, we begin to give ourselves away, and even though we want to do right, we sacrifice so much just to keep that man in our lives. Yes, we seek to please him, initially by the way we behave, including how we dress. We even prepare for the day in our minds prior to meeting him. In his presence, we seek to satisfy him by thinking twice about what we will say because we want to give him the impression that he is the one for us. We do this at the cost of openly rejecting what our Father commands us to do and how He instructs us to act.

Loneliness is very detrimental. For this reason, it is imperative that the ruffles in our lives are ironed out so that we can learn to live with them. In other words, identifying your ruffles means that you know your areas that need work. You are willing to allow God to press them out neatly so that you can be seen as His righteous child even though you still have the ruffles of your past. As you live your life, these ruffles might come into your thoughts to discourage you, but remember that you are forgiven. Ask God to show you the triggers that make you to feel lonely. Learning your triggers is an effective and preventative measure in helping you understand your ruffles. It helps you learn who you are and how you respond. Remember, your ruffles do not prevent God from loving you. It is only the enemy who tries to make you feel this way. God loves you in spite of your ruffles.

Having our ruffles ironed out requires us to trust in God. We say we trust God, but do we? Do we really trust Him today to fulfill His promises? If we are honest, the answer is most likely no. Truthfully, if we trusted God, then many of us would be virgins. If you are not married or if you have not been married, then you should be a virgin unless someone took advantage of you. If this is the case, hopefully you sought counsel and know that there is no shame in what happened to you. You are loved by God, and He is able to heal you. You just need to trust Him. However, for the rest of us, we should be virgins who are waiting for the man that God will send us. That is the way things are supposed to be, but we often get lost in the moment of loneliness. We say that we trust God. However, what do our actions really say? Maybe our actions at church portray that we will hold on and wait on the Lord. Maybe some of us don't even pretend while at church. We wear the most seductive outfits and openly flirt with every man we see. We smile way too long at the brothers, and we hold a glance with them that does not say, "Let's have Bible study." I'm sure you know exactly what I am talking about. As believers, we have to be cautious of how we dress and how we maneuver while worshiping God. You know that church member who you think of and want to sit next to because he gives the best hugs ever? You have a wrinkle in your ruffles. Let God iron it out. Start by being mindful of your ways and consider what God expects of us.

Honestly, I don't like all that hugging in church. Firstly, some people don't wash their hands. Furthermore, not everyone is in the same frame of mind when they shake your hand or hug you. Do you know why I know? One time, I was taken to a different place during a meet-and-greet session at church. On this particular Sunday, I was sitting next to a well-dressed, good looking man. Initially, I had not paid any attention to him until the meet-and-greet time. The hug I received from this man during the meet-and-greet time made me feel comfort and satisfaction as if I were wanted by him. It was one of the best hugs I have ever received from a man. Yes, it happened at church. I can still feel him embracing me as he held me tightly. No, he did not run his hands down my back, but he held me. At that moment, I thought, I wish my husband held me like this. The effect of his hug became the object of my desire to the point where I looked for him several Sundays afterwards so that I could sit next to him, but he was nowhere to be found. For this selfish reason, I am now saying, "Nope. I don't like your hugs because those hugs can cause one to sin in their mind." You know that lust is a sin formed in our minds by our thoughts. When we think those thoughts, we already need to grab our inner phone line and hit our Father up to ask for forgiveness.

Some of you reading this will think, *Well, this girl has a serious problem.* If you think this is serious, you should keep reading. This is just a little icing. By the way, yes, I did have a serious problem, and I still have to be very careful of how I behave. I have to be careful of my thoughts and I have to be mindful of my dress. It all plays a part in the ability to be seductive and attract the wrong spirits into my life. I want to know who God is, and I want Him to speak to me daily so that when He corrects me, I can repent immediately. I do stumble sometimes and visit the land of "Get Back Here Before You Indulge", but I am learning my triggers, so I do not stay there as long as I used to. It is so good to catch myself when the Holy Spirit speaks to me, because when I do, I am reminded that I am not such a Christian who is not guilty of sin.

My flesh has to be put in check daily more times than you can imagine. That's me being real, and I know there are those who listen to the Holy Spirit daily. Good – then you will see where you need to work on improving yourself. I am simply sharing my struggle so that someone will know that God still loves them; He honestly loves people who have done wrong when they knew they were wrong. God loves everyone who has tried to get things right, even if they have failed several times. This walk with Jesus is one that requires daily subjectivity to follow His plan for our lives, because the enemy and his sidekicks are always ready to aim thoughts into our minds. They are schemers who seek to implement into you what they have learned about you; they plant seeds of doubt like a farmer in the spring. Sometimes, they even plant untruths mixed in with a few misguided facts. Let me give you an example on how Satan spreads the wildfire of lies.

If you are a gossiper, then you probably love social media. You probably always find time to be on the internet, looking up the latest about everything and everyone. When someone shares with you hot and juicy tips about someone else, you feel like you need to chime in with what you know about the person or what you think you know. However, do not think that God is not speaking to you too, and do not think you are living a sinless life, because that thought alone is one that causes Jesus to look at you with a double take. His Word says we all have sinned and fallen short of His glory (see Romans 3:23). Stop being indignant by saying that the Word says *"have* sinned" as if it is a thing of the past. I am glad you noticed the perfect past participle. Now, tell me what Jesus said about being evil and knowing how to give good gifts to your children (see Matthew 7:11). Are you calling Jesus a liar? He did not say, "you who *used to be* evil", He said, "you who *are* evil". We are referred to as being evil because of our sinful thoughts and our sinful ways, but we are covered by the blood of Jesus. Therefore, we are righteous. These thoughts of evil and righteous might seem to contradict each other, but Jesus is saying even in our sinful nature we seek to do good for our children. Our sinful nature is why we must put on the whole armor of God so that we can live under our supernatural protection given to us by Jesus. When we do not live under this protection, we live a sinful life. Yet even in our sin, we seek to do good deeds for those we love. Jesus is the key to us being righteous or evil. Faith in Him saves believers. If you believe that Jesus came to us from His heavenly Father, then your sins are covered. No one is better than the other person, because we all have areas in which we battle with thoughts or behaviors that do not follow the principles of God.

Our Father loves us so much and He wants us to live in peace. He even promised us that we will inherit the kingdom of God, and we have. The kingdom of God is the presence of the Holy Spirit in us (see Romans 14:17). We have a responsibility to share this good news with others. To share this good news, we must search the Scriptures so that we can have a better revelation of our Father. Do you know why? When we spend time studying scriptures, we will receive a message from God, because the Holy Spirit will give us the interpretation of the Word. Our Father's words can tell us what to do so that our future days will be far better than our past ones (see Job 8:7, Jeremiah 30:18, and Haggai 2:9). Listening to God's Word gives us insight on what we need to do so that we can be ready for the next level that He has for our lives. His word will tell us how to prepare for the spiritual war that we are in. Yes, we are in a war – a war in which many of us have a tendency to leave our armor in unknown places so that when the battle comes to us, we are seeking our shield of faith and desperately looking for the breastplate of righteousness. However, we are walking in our flesh with the spirit of anger or temptation. Because we have laid all our armor down, we start to act like non-believers.

Many times, I have had to search to protect my loins – not lions – with truth (although a lion would have done a better job of keeping the men away than I did). For now, let me focus on the significance of protecting our loins. Our loins are the areas where our sexual organs are located. So, there have been many years in which the only truth that was going for me was my craving for sex. Why? I loved sex, and sex ruled me. There was no effort on my part to deny this truth. My family and friends were exposed to the men in my life, but they never really knew how my craving had grown out of control, perhaps because my behavior was seen as normal. However, as I have actively read God's Word so that I can gain understanding, I realize that I was a member of the church of Thyatira (see Revelation 2:18-25). These verses reference how the church of Thyatira tolerates Jezebel. Yes, I was tolerating Jezebel's spirit, and her spirit spoke to me for many years without me recognizing what was happening. If you notice in the scripture, it says we are doing her ways. We are not even doing things our way, we have fallen and become under the submission of her ways when we sin sexually. Whether it is with a man or a woman, it is all wrong and places us under a spirit of darkness. A man just happened to be who I enjoyed sexually. Correction – *men* were who I enjoyed. As I continued to delight and please myself sexually, I knew when the spirits were on me. With each encounter where I felt their presence, I welcomed them. I strongly felt their presence and submitted to them while in the bed, when I seduced the man to do as I desired, or when I allowed him to please me.

While submitting to Jezebel's ways, I learned what men enjoyed, and I took delight in making them crave me only to walk away when I chose. Walking away was extremely easy, especially when they were not good in bed. I did not think about their self-esteem nor their wants. Yes, that was me. I loved sex then (and I still do), but now, I am more cautious of how I behave when I am around men, and since I am aware of my cravings,

I always keep my best friend with me. Honestly, I don't even trust myself to go anywhere without Him – the Holy Spirit. I have to listen to Him because He tells me if the person has ill intentions or if I have them. If I am honest, I don't even deal with too many people for too long because I don't want us to have thoughts that are outside the boundaries of Christian love.

I know there are those who will read this and think, *I am going to keep her away from my husband.* Well, I don't want him anyway. As a matter of fact, I never sought married men. They sought me, but there were only three occasions during my early years in which I slept with a married man. Now that I am delivered and my flesh is under the submission of God, the Holy Spirit comforts me. God checks my thoughts and I submit them to Him. I understand if you think you need to protect your man by keeping him away from me and women like myself, but know this – it is best to pray for your marriage and ask the Holy Spirit to give you insight and wisdom on how to deal with that situation, because if you deal with it in a fleshly way, you might incite a war that you are not prepared to handle.

In the battle, being armed with no more than your mouth and threats only fans the flames. Being prayerful at all times for yourself and your family will give you the victory during any spiritual battle. Being armed with the Word of God, speaking scriptures over your family, and praying have the best effect. When we fail to pray for our family and speak positively to our husbands like God commands, the outcome can be detrimental. Attitude matters, as it greatly impacts our ability to persevere. Staying prayerful at all times, ask God to guide you and stay equipped for the battle with the right weapons.

Ruffles also exist in our families. Spiritual war is always seeking to divide our family, so God has taught me not to identify my concerns about His behavior when He is telling me His concern. How often do we do this? When someone is expressing how they feel, we take it as an opportunity to give them a piece of our minds. Instead, we need to accept correction so that we can work on being more Christ-like and ask God to give us direction on when we can share our concerns about that person. Be ready to hear, "Never," or, "Not now." It's all a part of learning from God.

Can we prepare for battle? Yes, that is what David did. Prior to fighting Goliath, he killed a bear and a lion. He had this experience, and his prior knowledge helped him defeat Goliath. We need to use what we have to defeat the enemy. Like David, we can be victorious too. First, we need to identify what God has given us to defeat the principalities. How can we be ready for war or any "Goliath" that world sends after us? Our armor will help us. To be ready, we have to prepare for battle. Notice that the Bible says to put on the full armor of God. That means we have to take action to have the armor on. We are not gifted with the armor to the point in which it is put on us. We must spiritually put on the armor to be protected so that we can be ready for this spiritual war.

Because God said to put on the full armor, it also means that we can take it off at our leisure. When we do not want to be covered or protected, we take off our armor. We do this so we can do what we want to do. This decision to step away from our protection that God has given us so that we can enjoy sin sets us up to be defeated. As we indulge in our sinful ways, we begin to enjoy sin more and more. Our actions put us under the submission of the one who wants us to disobey God: Satan. If you remove your armor, you are rolling with Satan and his crew. Notice that He warns us to keep our armor on so that we can be ready for the day of evil. He did not say "just in case" evil comes; He said *when* evil comes.

Sometimes, as Christians, we seem to believe that we will not be under attack, but please know that evil is coming. If you are a child of God and you think, *Well, the devil doesn't bother me*, trust me, he knows who you are. I want to tell you that Satan knows everything about you because he has studied you, and if you are not bothered by him, you are both on the same team. There is no way you can be of Christ and not be pestered by this spirit that denies God.

Now, here is the part that many of us struggle with – we put on the armor of God, but we do not want to stand still. We need to be able to stand still. Why? That is all God is calling us to do. He is not saying to slap the devil with our words, because he knows our tongues spill out evil thoughts, and evil words come at the time when we should be standing on the Word of God and remaining silent. Implement your Miranda rights. Close your mouth. Get your Bible out, put a scripture on that warfare, and pray. That is how we stand, knowing that God's Word is true and does not fail (see Joshua 23:14). By knowing that God's Word does not fail, we know that all we need to do is not engage until God gives us direction to. Now, while you are standing on the Word – not advancing with your mouth or with your sword ready to pierce the person in the side – God just wants you to stand on the Word by trusting it. Take your flesh out of the equation and stand firm on the Word of God by implementing scriptures while you are under attack. Standing requires us to seek time to spend with God daily. Spending time with God is no longer happenstance; it is a deliberate effort by you that is established so you can develop your relationship with your Father.

While standing, we need to read and meditate on the word of God. This does not mean we are telling every friend about our problems. Stop talking about the problem. Your words are breathing life to the problem, not to the resolution that God has for you. Besides, most of the time, your friends really don't want to hear about your issues anyway, and others are only listening so that they can gossip. Listen: let me help you identify the ones you need to be cautious of speaking to during wartime. Listen to what they say. If they egg you on to do things that are not of God, stop talking and stop listening. If they agree with your vindictive plan of doing something foolish, stop talking and stop listening. If they say, "Girl, I would if I were you," stop talking and stop listening. You are not standing, you are gossiping and seeking other means of resources to help comfort you while you are at war. You are seeking a solution that is not God-centered or God-focused. Just because you are standing on the Word doesn't mean that things will get better instantly, because God reiterated the importance of just standing. Now, let's get our armor ready for the battle. Hopefully you will keep it on, because the war is real.

Free Tip!

By the way, when you read about the church of Thyatira, it references eating idols' food. You might think, *I don't eat food that is sacrificed to idols*, but do you frequent businesses that boldly sacrifice to their idols? I have, and when we do this, we are under the spirit of Jezebel. Unless you are visiting those businesses for Christian discipleship, then you need to reevaluate where you do business. This is especially true if you are not tithing, because when you consider that you are not giving to your God but are instead giving to false gods, you are denying our God. He does not like that at all (see Exodus 34:14). In case you are wondering how you give to their gods, consider that they are taking the money that you are paying for their services and they use those funds to buy food for their gods. Stop supporting their gods.

We are at war, whether you realize it or not, and we need to identify who the real enemy is. Not knowing what is going on does not prevent you from being in a battle. You, my sister, are at war against spirits – a war that you have no idea how to deal with if you think you can handle it with your emotions, because your emotions and your feelings will betray you. The enemy has studied you, so he knows how to get you off track. He knows how you think and how you respond to certain situations. Ephesians 6:10 says that we are fighting a real war. We are fighting a war that is not against people. It is a spiritual war. Yes, people are used in this fight. People are used in this war to get you distracted, and you know that there are many battlefields in the war.

Let me help you identify where you are at war. You can be at war in your marriage, because Satan does not like this unity of God. You can be at war at your job, because Satan wants Christians to look and act like the rest of the world. He does not want us to minister to others. You can be at war even while driving. I know this is an area in which I often find myself thinking, *Oh my God, hurry up and provide so I do not have to drive!* Honestly, I enjoy riding the bus because I do not have to deal with traffic. There are times in which I desire a driver. For instance, one day, while riding the bus, I was busy doing things that I wanted to do to get my day in order, and I nearly missed my stop. However, the Holy Spirit helped me realize this early enough so that I could arrive at church on time. Bus riding does not hurt me. I enjoy it, but I would love the quick drive to the market to get a few things. However, driving requires me to pay closer attention. If I am honest, I tend to break the law. Yes, I am being honest, and if you drive, you will admit that you break the law too. Let me refresh your memory – texting and driving, slowing down at stop signs instead of stopping, speeding when you want to get someplace more quickly, and of course, while this does not technically count as breaking the law, don't forget the angry thoughts and commonly used rude gestures that you direct towards other drivers who make you angry. These are all harmful actions that we need to discontinue – even running yellow lights. If you encounter any of these issues, that is a war zone for you, too.

How we respond makes the greatest impact on the world and on our walk with God with Him in full control. Those spirits know how you will respond in each of these situations. They study you more than you study yourself. Dr. Charles Stanley created a method of recognizing when we are most likely to be under attack with an acronym called HALT. The spirits of darkness come after us when we are hungry, angry, lonely, and tired (HALT). These are the times when I am most vulnerable, and it seems that my son always catches me at one of these times. I know because I used to say things to him like, "Son, why are you asking me this while I am hungry?" Sometimes, I would say, "Why are you asking me this while I am tired?" One day, he caught me off guard with his response. He said, "Mom, are you always hungry and tired?" *Bam!* I was a Christian called out for her bad behavior. Most of the time, when my son talks to me, it is in the evening. To solve this problem, I would try to eat before he came home from school, or, when he talked to me, I would remember his words. Was I always in a position for the prince of darkness to intervene in my life, and would I always allow him to have his way? Thankfully, now I would say, "Not always," but there was a time when I would have had to say, "Most of the time."

CHAPTER 5

My "I Love Sex" T-Shirt

There is no way that I can lie to anyone. I thoroughly love sex. It was part of my life; having a sex partner or two who could provide multiple orgasms made life pleasurable. I didn't actually own a t-shirt with the words "I love sex" on it, but my behavior exhibited my true thoughts. Sex was part of how I felt empowered when dealing with men. My dependence on having multiple orgasms and their ability to provide them was my main goal. Sure, I could dwell on those intimate moments so that you could see how much I loved sex, but those thoughts trigger the craving inside of me, so just trust me when I tell you that I needed to be reformed by God. In the search for reformation, I found my armor, which allowed me to stop lying and manipulating to get what I wanted.

The part of the armor that I had to really locate and identify was the armor of truth that protects your sexual organs. The reason it references protecting your loins in this manner is because during Paul's days, men wore a tunic. As you can imagine, they are extremely long, and it would be very difficult to maneuver while wearing the tunic during war. Therefore, men would tie their tunic up around their waist, and this allowed them to move freely during battle without restriction. As we review what Paul is saying, I believe he wants us to understand that the sexual battles we face require us to take action. He knew that we need to make an intentional effort to protect our sexual organs so that we would not sin against God. If you take notice, these weapons represent tangible items that we can simply pick up and use. To protect us from engaging in sex, we need to gird our loins with truth (see Ephesians 6:14 KJV) In the process of girding our loins or protecting ourselves, the way in which you tie the tunic indicates that it not only allows you to maneuver, but it also prevents you from having access to your sexual parts. In the process, you are exposing one part of your body – your legs – but you are preventing access to the other part of your body. Simply put, we might become exposed to sin, but implementing God's plan protects us.

So, even though we are exposed to the spirits that want us to engage sexually, we are protected because we have taken steps to prevent our sexual organs from being available. In other words, the spirits can see, and they know what you like, whether it is a man or a woman. However, because you have taken action, you are not exposed to where they can readily get at you. Still, we must take other physical actions besides simply picking up something to protect our sexual organs. "Stand therefore, having your loins girt about with truth" (Ephesians 6:14, KJV). I believe that God is telling us that we need to arm our sexual organs with the truth of God's Word, which tells us we should not have sex outside of marriage or when we are not married nor commit any sexual acts with individuals of the same sex or with animals.

God's Word is one truth that we need to keep in our mind and follow, especially since our mind which is part of our soul can be deceived. We also need to listen to the spirit of truth, because He will help us keep our armor on. The spirit of truth will remind us that we are not following the rules established by God to protect us. Before we engage in any sexual acts, He will speak to us.

CHAPTER 6

Don't Scuff Up Your Easter Shoes

Why would my mother ever think I was girly enough to wear a pair of white patent leather shoes without getting them all scuffed up? I was dressed for failure from the moment they hit my feet, because I was the only daughter who thought that all shoes were running shoes. Add to the mix that I had to keep these shoes on for hours before being released to change them, and you can probably imagine what they looked like at the end of the day – a true replica of a zebra's stripes.

Remember when I told you earlier that I spent countless hours in church? I often wished I could be outside with my neighbors, who never went to church except on occasions like Easter or funerals. With this attitude, I spent many Sundays reluctantly sitting in church, being in attendance but not attentive, especially on holidays like Christmas. I still recall sitting by the space heater and being one of the two children who came to church. Don't get excited and think, *At least she had someone to play with,* because the only other child that was there was my sister Monica. The deacons did not even require their children to come to church. Go figure.

Like the other children who were all at home having a good time, I wanted to play with my toys too. With my selfish, childlike mindset, I did not recognize that the only reason I was able to have those things was because of God; neither did I realize the impact that simply being in attendance at church would have on my life. So, when I went off to college to be free of my parents' watchful eye, the pride of life had already planted a seed that took root and grew.

Over time, I began to realize that I unknowingly behaved more selfishly because the spirit of pride had become part of me, and the actions I took were based on my soul's desire to live the life that appeared to be the best life – the life that many enjoy, laugh about, and talk about. I did not realize that I was in a spiritual battle, and it took my heavenly Father's insight to help me understand the challenges I encountered and why. For this reason, I am forever grateful for my Father's presence, because He is the only one who could love me in the dreadful condition that I was in.

Even though I have made changes to live in the righteousness of God, I know that the ways in which I try to live as He directs still require me to repent daily for my actions. This was not my attitude before at all. I always thought that it was the other people who needed to repent, because I was in far better shape than them. You know, I was the one with the beam in my eye causing me not to see the truth about my Father and how I was not representing the family at all. For this reason, I can truly say that our Father really loves us and He wants us to overcome every battle with His insight. Our willingness to change either slows down, speeds up, or prohibits our progression to enjoying a life free of bondage.

When we realize that we are in bondage or slaves to Satan, a shift is needed. Escaping bondage should immediately become a craving that tempts you more than a peanut brownie with ice cream. We have to transform our mind (see Romans 12:2). The most powerful aspect of my transformation happened when I fell in love with God. Falling in love with God allowed me to embrace God's love for me. It transformed my mind from having a very selfish, uncaring demeanor into one in which I commit time to learn of Him. I am excited to wake up in the morning and share the day with His presence. Just like in the physical world, when we love someone, we want to spend time with them. The same is true with our Father, so I began to spend time with Him. I began to fill my mind with His thoughts as I read the word of God (see Colossians 3:16). When I stopped thinking like the world, I stopped feeling guilty for my past, because God does not want us to become overwhelmed with guilt. He cares so much for us and wanted us to be redeemed to the extent that He allowed His only Son to sacrifice His life for us. Our Father sending Jesus to come to earth for us means so much, as it was a seed (see Genesis 3:15 KJV), and like any seed, when we accept it by planting it in good soil, it grows and becomes fruitful. Jesus, the seed, was sent to redeem us so that we could enjoy life without the bondage or slavery of sin.

When we read our Bible, that is where we will find out the truth about how much our Father really loves us. Before falling in love with God, spending time reading the Bible was definitely not in my daily, weekly, or monthly plans. Now that I understand the power of the written Word, I want to encourage you to get out your sword. That is right – your Bible is a sword. We all know the power of a sword in battle. This sharp weapon is used to slash and thrust your enemy into defeat, but in order for this to happen, we – the soldier – must know how to use it.

I know many of you are like me when you get a new gadget – you prefer to figure out how to use it on your own instead of reading the owner's manual. We even apply this method to our Christian lives. As a result, we have been slaughtered by the enemy in our thoughts and actions. My advice to you is to stop losing the battle and give Satan the beating of his life. When you are ready to defeat the enemy, get your weapon out – the word from our Father – and use it! Stop allowing Satan to defeat you with his manipulative ways. He has stolen enough from us, and it is our time to get it back. The best defense is to stop allowing Sunday to be the only time you get the Word from God. Sunday gatherings are for us to encourage each other, but the best way to encourage each other is with the Word of hope, which is from our Father (see Hebrews 10:25). Because I got tired of getting beaten when I knew that God had better, I returned to God so that He could fulfill His purpose in me (see Psalm 57:2).

When you begin your journey towards walking in your Father's love, one of the most important points that I truly want you to understand is that we are not in a physical battle, no matter who seems to be attacking you. They are not the enemy, as Satan has been hiding behind this truth for the longest time, causing division among so many. Instead, see things as God directs us to see them and accept that we are in a spiritual battle (see Ephesians 6:12). These spirits enjoy jumping into our bodies to possess us. Perhaps you think that possession is too strong of a word, but when you relinquish your power to these spirits, they want to take complete control of your every action. That's possession!

Have you ever done something and wondered why you did it? It was probably something that was completely uncharacteristic of your behavior. You might have even felt guilty or shameful of your behavior afterwards. This unprecedented behavior happened because of dark spirits who enter in and make suggestions that we often quickly follow, especially when we are angry, hungry, or frustrated. They take advantage of our emotions, as they know that these are times in which we are more likely thinking only of ourselves. These spirits might even come into others and have them make suggestions about what we should do so that we entertain these seeds planted into our thoughts. When we encounter these situations, we might act unlike our Father would prefer us to act. These acts are the beginning of the dark spirits possessing you to manipulate you.

Why are these demonic spirits so determined to find a home in our bodies? It is because they no longer have a body. They are seeking our bodies so that their wills can be fulfilled (see Matthew 12:45). If we consider that Satan's fallen angels used to have bodies during the time of Noah, as they saw earthly women as beautiful and had children with them (see Genesis 6:2), we will begin to understand their yearning to set up home in our bodies. Their intent is to do harm to God through us – through manipulation, deceitfulness, and distractions, in any way possible.

The good thing is that we know that they have already been defeated by our Father, so we have the right to give them an eviction notice without proceedings. When we evict them, we need to be mindful that they will be upset; some spirits will go out and come back only to find things in order (see Luke 11:25-26). This shift angers the spirits, so they may attempt to go and get seven more wandering spirits who are more evil than themselves to try to take over us. To defeat them, we must be armed and ready with the Word of God. Otherwise, if they find us empty of the Word, the seven demons could become your new house guest. Arm your soul, which includes your mouth, your mind, and your heart with the Word of God and say what God says when you feel yourself under pressure of any kind. Trust that God's Word is true and live knowing that you are victorious because you are fighting the good fight of faith, and that is a fight in which you have already won.

CHAPTER 7

Fighting in Heels

In every way, I sought to please my flesh, which allowed spirits of darkness to dwell in me. I basically said, "Jezebel spirit, come on down. You are welcome in my body." I know it might sound crazy, but that was my attitude when I chose to walk in the life that was pleasing to me. Sexual immorality was the sin that was going to send me straight to hell (see Revelation 2:20-23). It all started with fornication, which later led to adultery, where my household spiritual guest led me to enjoy multiple orgasms to keep me distracted. Who am I kidding – I enjoyed it.

As life presented opportunities, I never saw these spirits as what they were: spirits who brought more spirits who sought to show me the satisfaction of my flesh, my eyes, and my pride. These spirits overlooked my efforts to act as a Christian. They were not bothered by my church attendance, as this had been my pattern since a child. Going to church on Sunday, sending my son to Christian school, and listening to gospel music were mere actions, as they did not reflect my love for my Father. Like many Christians, these spirits are fine with our pretense to be like our Father. It is not until we become one with our Father that they realize that we are free of their manipulation. For this reason, these spirits did not mind me dressing in my Sunday's best to attend church because I made no attempt change my sexual lifestyle, which meant I welcomed their presence in my life.

If I am being honest, I even welcomed the spirit of prostitution. You see, at some point in my life, I thought I wanted to be a prostitute. This thought entered my mind as a child from television, as prostitution was presented as a glorious way of life. That is the danger of television, especially for our children, as Satan plants all kinds of thoughts in their minds that later take root and grow. Thoughts are powerful, because I even fantasized about standing on a corner and having the man I was dating come to pick me up off the corner. There were times in which I had him pretend to pick me up from a bar. Just the thought of standing on a corner looking for a man to pay for sex was dangerous, but it was a thought that was glamorized by the possessions that prostitutes often got from men. Remember, Isaac thought the men would kill him because of Rebekah, so he told them that she was his sister (see Genesis 26). He had a selfish thought that could have put his wife's life and other men's lives in danger had they slept with her. We need to be mindful of our thoughts and put them under Christ (see 2 Corinthians 10:5). We also need to be very mindful of the type of entertainment that we allow our children to watch.

A perception I received as a child grew and became part of my actions. When these actions transpired, I put others in danger. My selfishness and thought of prostitution led me to welcome this spirit into my life. No, I did not stand on a corner to wait on men to drive by to pick me up, but I embraced this lifestyle through my interactions with men. You see, I had several men in my life who would provide financial gifts, including funds for vacations, house repairs, birthday parties, phone bills, and insurance. You get the picture. That was prostitution, even though I wanted to look at it as simply having a man who took care of me. I was really prostituting myself for my benefit, because there were two men who did not want to provide finances, and I discontinued talking to them. If they wanted my time, they paid with finances. However, I did not like men who gave me money for sex. I recall one guy who gave me money on our first encounter. I never saw him again. I guess in my mind, there were only certain levels of prostituting myself that I would allow. Crazy, isn't it?

Please understand that these things happened because of *my* feelings and *my* wants. I was demonized by spirits that had taken control of me because I refused to transform my mind. I was not helpless in the act. I chose to allow them to be a part of me. I invited them into my life, and until I surrendered to God, this was my way of doing things. Prior to surrendering, my life was heading down a road of destruction in which I was no longer beginning to recognize myself. I recall one encounter with these demons. I could sense their presence, and I loved it. I felt extremely sexy, and the guy that I was with was capable of providing me sexual satisfaction that entire day. I did not care about him needing to work. I just wanted him to please me. Notice the pronoun "I". *I* was the problem, and when the Holy Spirit spoke to me several days later, my life began to change.

As time passed, while in this mindset, I was smoking more and more weed to prevent myself from hearing what the Holy Spirit was saying. There were times where I initially began to smoke weed and the Holy Spirit would tell me to stop smoking, even when I was high. He often warned me that it was going to be harder and harder for me to stop. To prove Him wrong, I would quit for a while, then pick the habit back up. When I reached the point where it was a daily habit, I knew there was a problem, because no matter how much I smoked, I could not get high enough to keep the Holy Spirit quiet. I wanted to get high so that I could enjoy multiple sexual orgasms (at least, that was my excuse). I thought the sex was only the greatest if I was high because it was easier for me to be pleased.

One night, I was standing in the bathroom smoking weed when I looked at myself in the mirror and I heard the Holy Spirit say, "Stop smoking." Immediately, I knew I had to stop, because it was not a suggestion, but a command with a sense of urgency. You know how your earthly father will tell you to stop doing something and you just keep on doing it, but when his voice changes, you know that he means business? That is how it was on that day. If I had not listened, I do not have a doubt in my mind that those demons were going to demand more of me, including stronger drugs and erotic behavior so that I could enjoy moments of pleasure. If I had not stopped smoking, my life would have been drastically different.

Minutes after the Holy Spirit told me to stop smoking, you will never guess what happened. The very next words that came out of my sex partner's mouth as I walked into the bedroom were, "You need to stop smoking, because we used to have sex without you smoking." Do you see what happened? This message was so important for me to hear that my Father sent the very same message to me twice, both within minutes of each other. Now, you might question if this truly was the Holy Spirit, because the guy I was with was not a Christian, but remember that God can use anyone and everyone to get a message to us. Although this might have been a controlling spirit in him that made him agree to tell me to stop smoking, the point is that it was said at the right time, causing me not to question whether or not it was a message from God. As a matter of a fact, after the guy said stop smoking, he started trying to justify why he made this comment, because even to him I guess his words did not make sense.

Remember, a person can give a message from God and then in the same breath have a word from the enemy. If you doubt this, look at Peter in Matthew 16. First, Jesus tells Peter that He received knowledge from His Father in heaven (see Matthew 16:17), but a few scriptures later, Jesus tells Peter, "Get behind me, Satan" (see Matthew 16:23). You see, even in seconds we can go from saying what God says to being an instrument for Satan. We have to recognize that we are in a spiritual battle at all times. Unfortunately, because they have become so common, we are relaxed when these spirits of darkness are influencing us, and we do not recognize them for who they are. We live a life of deception. Thankfully, I heard my Father loud and clear, so I started to shift into being obedient to His will for my life by stopping smoking.

When we do not acknowledge these demons' existence, it allows them to continue to have a hold of our lives without being seen for who they are. They exist without being recognized, sort of like termites. You don't realize their presence until after they have eaten your home and caused extreme financial damage. At that point, when you realize their presence and the damage they have done, you call for help. Likewise, when you realize that you have been overcome by demons or that they are setting up camp inside you, call on your Father to help you. Furthermore, read the love letter He has given you. Read it and listen to the message that He has for you. Your love for Him will grow and your every thought will be of Him. You might have to read a scripture several times to get the understanding that He has for you, but just do it. It will help mend your brokenness and it will help you become more like His child. You will want to do what He asks you to do, and you will change from being selfish to being more caring.

Let me tell you this little secret, so pay close attention: guilt, unforgiveness, shame, rejection, unworthiness, and discontentment are just a few of the things Satan will use to try to make you feel like a nobody. He wants to push you into behaving the way you used to behave and think. Grab your heels and know that you are who God says you are. Associate yourself with others who are walking with Christ and receive healing. Cling to the One who has the power to heal and know that

He will deliver you. Live knowing that you are free from bondage. You are delivered. Stay strong by replacing all Satan's negative thought suggestions with words of love and encouragement. If you must tell yourself these things one million times a day, do it, because it is true. Your Father loves you, and He heals the broken-hearted. His love will set you free from all the foolishness and lies that Satan throws at you. Fight knowing God heals and you will be victorious.

CHAPTER 8

Reject Guilt & Constantly Learn Without Condemnation

Galations 6:7 (NIV) states, "Do not be deceived: God cannot be mocked. A man reaps what he sows." Every time I hear someone reference this scripture, it is always in a negative way. "You did bad, so now you will reap a bad harvest." This scripture means so much more. It references the opportunity to change and follow God. God wants us to love Him and to allow Him to be present in our lives. He wants us to be aware of His presence, and He pays attention to how we live. God wants us to be honest with ourselves, because we truly cannot deceive Him by going to church every Sunday while living a life of disobedience every second that we are not at church. That was my life, and once I really said, "God, please forgive me," and allowed Him to really enter into my presence, things changed. No, I do not look differently physically. However, I am under the covenant of grace. I am forgiven for my sins, and I am not living under condemnation, and neither are you when you ask forgiveness. This means Satan can't condemn you with his suggestions of unworthiness, because you are forgiven.

Because I have accepted that I am forgiven, the seeds I plant now are not seeds that lead to destruction. I believe that once you change your life and start doing as God has instructed, things will change for you too. You are planting good seeds into the ground when you help someone. That is a good seed that will produce a good harvest. When you smile at someone, that is a good seed. When you ask for forgiveness, God will not say that you aren't forgiven and that you are still going to reap heartache, pain, and poverty all by yourself because you did bad things before you submitted your life to Him. He told the lady to go and that her sins were forgiven in Luke 7:48, meaning she did not have to condemn herself for her past mistakes, and no one else could talk trash to her either. She was free to live a godly life.

Now, don't think that because you have changed, people won't talk crazy to you and remind you of your old habits. The thing is, when they do it now, you will know you are forgiven. It is like a shield is in front of you – their words will bounce off because you know in your heart that they are describing the *old* you. Don't worry – there will still be people who will not be convinced that you have changed. That is not your battle. Allow God to work with them while you continue doing as God instructs you.

Yes, there are things that we will have to deal with because of the past decisions that we made, but when we deal with them, we will have God to guide us on how we should move forward. That is so awesome to know, because in the past, it was just me trying to figure out what to do. Now, I have my superpower helping me – the Holy Spirit. With His insight, victory is evident, and His insight into the situation can result in a miraculous ending. We simply need to take action and follow God's instruction. I know I have made mistakes, but it is so good to know that I have someone who really loves me and wants the best for me. He cares about my life so much and His very presence creates an ending that I can hardly wait to share.

When someone does us wrong, we often say she or he will "reap what they have sown". Is this a form of judgement that we are trying use to curse the person? The Bible encourages us to pray for those who misuse us. Besides, I don't have time to spend judging or cursing others. Why? God will redeem us. I do not want to spend my quality time thinking of the bad things that should happen to a person. I need to use every second I have working on me, because the more understanding I get regarding how God wants me to live, the closer I get to His promises being fulfilled in my life.

So, when we read this scripture, see it as one of increase. See it as a scripture requiring us to change. See this scripture as an opportunity to inherit the promises of God. We will reap good things in our lives because we trust in the Lord, so plant good seeds into the ground of faith. If we mess up, which I am sure we will, then we must simply ask God to have mercy and forgive us. The end. It is important for us to understand that God forgives in order for us to move forward.

In life, I am learning daily about things I should do. I have also done things that I should not have done, but in the process of learning, I ask God to open my ears to help me see and help me do better. When God reveals to me my issue, I learn and move forward. I do not sit and condemn myself with negative words or thoughts. This dangerous technique is one that many of us practice. Sometimes, I catch my mind saying negative things, and I have to say "No! I am successful and I am making good decisions. I will be able to overcome it because God is with me."

Negative thoughts will come, and when they do, we need to replace them immediately with positive thoughts. If you really want to stop negative thoughts from coming, replace them with a scripture. Over time, when that thought comes, you will automatically replace it with the Word, and it will cease to bother you in the way it once did. Now, I am not saying that it will never come again. I am saying that we must train our mind not to look at the circumstance and become emotionally attached, because this is when the bad thoughts can develop in our mind. Instead, we must look to God for direction. Keep thinking positively based on who God says you are and train your mind to be under the submission of the Word.

Even while I am writing this, I am having to train myself not to look at my current circumstance. I am having to say to myself, "You did as the Holy Spirit led you, and He only tells you what to do based on what God tells Him." Trusting God during this season of planting would have been impossible in the past, but once I committed to follow God, I learned to hear His voice when He speaks to me; I have learned that if what I hear does not produce good, then those are not thoughts from God. God does not speak of my failures in a negative way to harm me. God does not tell me how horrible I am. God speaks with love and kindness because He knows where I am mentally in this battle. He knows that He is my strength and that I am trusting Him.

On my journey, I have missed the mark. In other words, I have not gotten everything right because of hastiness, so from this experience, I have learned that hastiness is a time for me to tell myself, "Wait, consult God before moving forward." If you take away nothing from this book, understand this: I am not perfect. I am nowhere near being perfect. I have serious flaws which God is working on in me so that I can encourage others. He is not working on me just for my benefit, He is working on me for His kingdom-building. If you think God does not want you in His kingdom, or that because you have messed up over and over again on the same thing there is no hope for you! Please understand that you are the exact person that God wants in His kingdom and that no one can make you feel bad about what you have done when you make the world aware of your flaws. Once you tell your story the way God instructs you, then you will save and encourage so many more.

Oh yes, one more important truth: you will feel so relieved when you tell people your story filled with your flaws. I know I do. I feel as if no one can say, "Oh, now you are walking with Jesus, but I remember when you used to smoke weed and you were sleeping with two men at once." For those who really know me, they would probably say, "Girl, no – she had three men at one time." You see, there is no one who can tell your story better than you, and there is no one who can condemn you for your past. You are redeemed by God. You are free from all bondage, so use your truth to save others who struggle with the same thing.

We have to get to the point in our lives where we accept all of who God says we are. We have to accept all that He has for us. I know that He wants me to do well and prosper according to 3 John 1:2. God wants us to prosper. In order to prosper, we must be willing to learn. I recall my journey as an entrepreneur. Initially, I had one level of eyesight for my business, but God sends us messages through others, and when we pray, He will enlarge our vision, according to 1 Chronicles 4:10. When you receive insight from God about how He will intervene in your life, trusting Him will guarantee that you will reach the destination quicker because He is like a secret agent. Do you know what I mean? God will give you inside information that will help you make decisions that will benefit your purpose. He will help you avoid pitfalls and ditches that others may try to convince you to step into, but because God is giving you guidance, He will safely show you the way.

I have met millionaires before, and I listened to them share how they made ten million dollars quicker than others on their journey to build a business. Immediately, I thought, *Oh wow, that is good. I want to learn from you. I am going to succeed by being under you.* However, we cannot succeed from being under others. Yes, mentors are good and helpful, but we need to be under

God. God will guide us and send the mentors that He wants us to have.

God told me, "You see how quickly she became wealthy? I did it for her. I can double it for you. You just need to follow my plan. Do not align yourself with anyone or anything that operates outside of my principles. My principles are in place for a reason. Do not get it twisted. You are here so that I can help you to see what is possible when you trust in Me and keep the faith. I will speak to you and show you a way that has not been done by others, and I can create opportunities that will reassure you that I am present in your life."

God is powerful. He is not afraid for you to hear His boldness. He will let you see things, and you will be like, "Yes!" Then, He will say, "Now that you are alone, let's work this out the way I have designed for you. First, align your flesh with me and don't get frustrated when others won't help you, because I have a ram in the bush." The scripture where God mentions the ram in the bush has to be one of my favorites (see Genesis 22:13). God always has a way of providing when we are in a situation where He has guided us to be and we cannot see how we are going to advance.

I have two dogs. When I walk them, I take two poop bags with me. Well, one day, as we walked in the neighborhood to get fruit from low-hanging trees, I took three bags. The third bag was for the fruit. As I was walking the dogs, both of them decided that they had to poop again. *Really?* I thought. I said, "God, where is my ram is in the bush?" Yes, I expected a poop bag to be a ram in the bush, too! I walked across the street, and not only was there a bag in the bush, but there was also was a bag floating behind the bush. I took the freely floating bag and smiled at the one in the bush. Joyfully, I walked across the street and picked up the poop. As I reflected on the bag in the bush, I walked home, knowing that God will supply all of my needs.

He will cause blessings to appear, we just need to acknowledge that God provided them. So, stay encouraged and know that God is with you. He wants you to succeed in life, and He will provide for you. Do not get caught up in your past, because your past can no longer hold you bondage. You are free to enjoy the ram in the bush. Keep believing, because God has a plan for you. If He cared enough to provide me a poop bag, you know that He cares about your life. Keep your eyes open for the ram in the bush, and ask God to give you insight; you just need to keep believing in His plan for your life. Most importantly, stop thinking other people are better than you. They are not. We are all heirs to the kingdom, so start listening to God the King so that you can enjoy His presence and favor in your life.

It is very important to realize that our Father wants to rescue us from every situation that we are in. Recognizing that we are out of relationship with Him is the first step toward our reconnection with Him. Because I realized how the power of God rescued me when I was walking around and doing more than simply scuffing up my Easter shoes, I have grown to know the importance of sharing my story. Prior to me realizing how scuffed up things were, like many, I thought I was destined to go to heaven simply because I went to church in my Sunday's best and believed in God. A reality check uncovered the truth: I was hell bound.

I know there are many who think that they are going to heaven even though they intentionally violate God's Word and participate in sins that God continues to warn us not to commit because they will send us to hell. It is important to tell my story because I want the world to know how forgiving our God is. God has set me free from all the guilt and shame that people may try to fill me with. Go ahead, say what you please, because I know I am forgiven. So, as you read my truth, embrace this truth which is our Father loves us. He does not hold us to worldly standards or to the worldly way of loving one another. His love is one that embraces us where we are and lifts us to where He wants to take us.

I have been delivered by God from these demons. I recognize that I had invited the spirits in with my lust for sexual satisfaction, and these spirits (see Matthew 12:43-45) were setting up camp. They had invited other demons to come like unwanted house guests. However, when we recognize that these spirits are only able to come because of invitation, we can evict them immediately by putting on our whole armor. That is why it is extremely important for us to have on the whole armor of God (see Ephesians 6: 11-18). While armored with the power of God, we begin to realize that Jesus first equipped his disciples with the ability to cast out spirits (see Matthew 10:1), so get to casting them out and fill that empty space with the love of God, because you are not powerless. You have the Spirit of God in you. That is your gift from your Father. Know the truth and study the Bible, which is our love letter from our Father. As you read the love letter, the Holy Spirit will reveal to you the truth in what the Lord is saying to you.

Because I am free, I want others to be free. Along this journey to healing and restoration, I wrote this book. Whether we believe it or not, we are destined to endure the second death if we do not change from our sinful lifestyle (see Revelation 21:8). I know I have said this before, but I want this point to be clearly understood because I have heard bishops and ministers comment that believers do not go to hell. They misinform their members, and this lie comforts them in their sinful life choices. This belief is one of the biggest lies that exist in the minds of believers because it allows so many to be deceived by the truth. Do not think that you or I can get to heaven and blame the minister for misinforming us, because the Bible tells us to search the scriptures (John 5:39-42). Do not try to tell our Judge that *He* is not being fair because of *our* decision not to study the Word. That is why we have it. We are to use it to block the firing darts of Satan. These fiery darts are going to send so many to hell, so we need to armor up and read the Word, because our Father warns us throughout the Bible to be very careful of our unpleasing behavior. It is not enough for Christians to think that they are going to heaven simply because they believe.

Look – read the scriptures for yourself. Notice how the demons responded to Jesus when they saw Him. They recognized Jesus (see Mark 1:34), and to recognize someone, you have to believe that they exist. You cannot recognize anyone that you do not know or that does not have existence. Secondly, they already know what their punishment is, and they have an idea when their rampage on earth will end, so for this reason, they asked Jesus if He had come early to deliver their end punishment. They know that Jesus will be the one to seal their ending. Notice that they did not try to repent for their behavior. Their response was focused squarely on themselves. That is the problem many of us have. We focus so much on ourselves that we not only miss what God is trying to tell us, but we also miss opportunities to be healed or delivered. We even miss opportunities to be a witness to others through our behavior and interactions with them.

Our behavior indicates that we need to transform our minds. To help transform our minds, there is a need to seek God by daily reading the Bible to find out who He really is. Our Father truly loves us. In order to find out more about His love, it is time for us to awaken and accept that God has given us insight on how we should live in love. He has warned us of the tricky demonic spirits and the treacherous devil. Breaking free from our selfish ways gives us an opportunity to embrace where we are and how we can go from our selfish thinking to godly thinking, because this world needs us to speak up and actually live the life we have pretended to live. This season of shaking has happened so that we can walk in the power of God and honor Him through His presence in our lives.

CHAPTER 9

Unfolding the Undergarment of Truth

Most of the time, when I am relaxing with the Holy Spirit, He gives me insight about myself – how I need to change and what I need to work on so that I can represent His kingdom. For years, my son has been telling me about my behavior. He has told me on numerous occasions that I do not know how to talk to people. It must have been pretty bad, because one day, while he and I were having Bible study, he gave me a scripture to read, which was Romans 12:9-22. Then, he asked me if I knew what it meant. In my mind, I was thinking, "He does not know the meaning of this scripture." However, the meaning is as plain as day. Later, after discussing these scriptures, I asked him if he understood it. His reply shocked me. He informed me that he knew what it meant, he just wanted to make sure I knew what it meant because he noticed that I treat people with indifference.

Of course, this was not his first time bringing my behavior to my attention. He would always tell me that I do not know how to talk to people from the hood (the inner city). My response was always defensive. I would say things like, "Boy, you do not know what you are talking about – I worked in inner city schools all twenty-two years of my teaching career." Besides, who was he to tell me about my attitude? He was the child, and I was the adult. I was supposed to be the one telling *him* about *his* issues. You get my point; my attitude was bad from the beginning. My mind was all like, *You can't tell me anything,* but God tells us that out of the mouths of babes, a fortress can be built to protect us from the adversary (see Psalm 8:2). In other words, my Father was using my son to give me insight about my ways. I was always reluctant to accept what he was telling me until the Holy Spirit told me on that very day that I had a problem. With the scripture in mind and with the desire to want to do right, I started paying attention to my actions, and I purposely paid more attention to how I responded to people.

A few days later, the Holy Spirit put me in a position of watchfulness to demonstrate how much I needed to focus on myself less so that He could become greater in my life. One day, I walked to the store to pick up a few items. For convenience, I wore my backpack so that I could just put all my items in it after paying for them when I walked back home without having to carry any bags. As I entered the store, I was greeted by the cashier, who informed me that I could not take my backpack into the store and that I would have to leave it at the front. Immediately, I gave her a look and said that I was not going to steal anything from the store. I further tried to justify myself by saying that I have been in the store before with my backpack and no one stopped me. Annoyed, I took out a few valuables from my backpack and left it at the front of the store. Let me back all the way up – I did not just take the things out; I took them out with an *attitude*. I treated them as if I thought *they* were the thieves. I even called out the names of each item that I thought was valuable as I took them out. Then, I gently slung the backpack to the place where she told me to place it and walked off grumbling. My attitude was all wrong, and although I tried to control my tone, it was evident that I did not agree with the policy and did not want to obey it. The frustration was quite visible in my face, my body language, my word choice, and my tone. My whole attitude was wrong.

As I walked to get the items I wanted from the store, the Holy Spirit softly said, "You are wrong. You cannot treat people like this." After gathering my shopping goods, I went to the cash register and apologized to the ladies, as they were just doing their job. It was not my responsibility to make their jobs harder with my attitude. Thankfully, they accepted my apology, and now I can go into the store not only with my backpack, but also with my two dogs leading the way. If I had not apologized, I am sure they would have asked me to leave my backpack at the front of the store and to leave my dogs outside. Just get this point – attitude is everything. We need to guard it because it shows and reflects the inner core of who we are.

To help me work on my attitude, I purposefully spend time with the Holy Spirit daily. The time I spend doing this reflects in my demeanor because I am more careful of the words that fly out of my mouth. Do not think I still won't fly off every once in a while, and I am in no way justifying my flying off, but I am saying that I am learning to know and do better. Because of the times in which my mind becomes conformed, I will act like the rest of the world. For this reason, we must renew our minds constantly. It is not a one-day renewal – it is a lifetime requirement. Since I recognize this now, I am working to improve the way I represent the kingdom of God daily. The situations I encounter might not look the same all the time, but they teach me valuable lessons.

For instance, I can recall the first time I visited a church that really worked on servicing people with issues such as drug and alcohol addiction. I was invited by a believer whom I met while riding the bus. As I walked onto the premises of the church ground, I looked at several people. The way they looked was hard to ignore. Their look said, "I barely made it to church, and I am struggling to hold it together." While walking past them towards the church's doors, my body began to tense. Immediately, God said to me, "These are my children. I love them too." With His words of love, I relaxed and shook their hands with a smile. In that instant, I realized that I do think more highly of myself than I ought to and that the only way to see people is through the eyes of love like my Father does. There was no difference between them and me. I was struggling just like they were, except I could hide my issues a little better behind my Sunday dress.

This attitude also made me see my dad in a different light, as he would often go to pick up members and bring them to church. He never allowed societal stigma to prevent him from serving others. I love my dad for that great memory. It gives me joy to reflect on his serving attitude so that I can be reminded that this is how we are to operate on earth. My Lord wanted me to know the value of everyone. He does not care about my social status, because to Him, we are all heirs to the throne. He cares about our lives, our hearts, and our willingness to love. We are all His children just as much as our own birth children are ours. You see, pride of life is a real issue. It exists on earth because it was an issue that Satan had in heaven. As a result, he no longer gets to reside in heaven with God. Instead, he uses pride of life to separate us from each other. We need to recognize this problem now so that we can stop causing, supporting, and engaging in conflicting issues that do not minister the message of love from our Father.

If you want to know how to get from being so selfish to hearing the truth about your ways that need rectifying, I advise you to spend time with the Holy Spirit if you want to change. I say this because if you do not want to change, you will not change. If you ask the Holy Spirit to help you and to show you how to live, He will. He will correct you through many ways. You just need to make sure you are ready to hear from Him. You can even listen to what others are telling you about your behavior and watch how you respond to their correction.

Attempting to justify your behavior is the first sign that you might need to revisit the situation, not just within your own thoughts, but with a heart that is willing to hear what the Holy Spirit has to say. After the church incident, I was like, "I get it, Lord – You love us all." I welcomed their presence at church, and I enjoyed worshipping with them. Mind you, I *had* to welcome their presence, because none of them seemed to have an issue with me being the stranger in the group visiting their church. Of course, you know my lessons are not over yet. Every day, I am learning how my prideful life choices create discrepancies among people and God's purpose.

Don't be so concentrated on your own plan that you end up missing out on God's plan. The other day, I flew to Texas. The trip turned out to be a quick "pop in and pop out" one. Although the business deal did not go as I had planned, it did go as God planned it. As I was heading back to the airport, I noticed that the next flight was leaving in forty-five minutes, so I wanted to catch that flight. When I arrived with thirty minutes until boarding, I rushed to the ticket counter. The attendants were just leaving, and I was not able to catch the flight. The next flight was boarding in eight hours, so I had to spend the night at the airport.

As I walked around, I tried to find an area that was close to a restroom with good lighting. After wandering around the airport for a bit, I located the closest restroom to the ticket counter that was not in the main way, so it would not be busy. I buckled down for the night and began reading my Bible. Now, this was the season in which the coronavirus pandemic warnings were issued, and while traveling, various rules about crowds were implemented. Honestly, with all the different reports, it was evident that no one really knew what was going on in regards to the pandemic.

With this in mind, I purposefully found a section that had several empty seats. The entire area was filled with about seven empty rows of seating. Then, this lady came to sit on the same row that I was on. Really? That was what I was thinking initially. However, I smiled and asked her if she missed her flight too. She glanced at me and said, "Oh no, I am going downtown." With that statement, I figured she was only sitting by me temporarily, so I felt better. However, when she began to put her socks on and get out her blanket and pillow, I realized that she was spending the night at the airport, too. Later, I looked across, saw another man, and immediately questioned whether he was traveling or not. He appeared as if he was holding it together, but his clothes could have used a good washing. I smiled at him and admired him, as his slender body and dark complexion reminded me of my dad. Within a few hours, another man came in, and I immediately thought, *This is the homeless section. What are they doing at the airport?*

However, before that thought could settle in my mind, God said to me, "These are my people. They deserve a warm place to sleep, too." With that thought, I calmed my nerves, but I also moved, because the lady was literally a few inches from placing her feet on my purse; she had stretched out on three seats while wrapped in her blanket. After adjusting myself into another corner, I relaxed and prepared to sleep for a few hours before going to the ticket counter. Just as I was laying down my head, this very loud lady came bouncing in. She had missed her flight, so she was video chatting with her male friend without her headphones. *Ugh,* I thought. I was just settling down – didn't she know that? I was not Christ-like at all. I said out loud, without warning and with an attitude, "Nobody wants to hear your conversation. Can't you see we are trying to sleep?" God spoke again. He told me that I have to learn to be tolerant of people because I don't know how many people have had to be tolerant of me.

Go figure. I have to tolerate others. I suppose that goes back to the scriptures my son had me read from the book of Romans. That is why I tell you to ask for the Holy Spirit to show you ways in which you do not represent the kingdom of God, because even when you think you are justified, He will point out your errors. It reminds me of the time when I turned in my first writing assignment in college and I thought it was a great piece, but when I got it back, it had red marks all over it. My professor even wrote "You are the death of my red pen" on my paper. It was the same feeling when the Holy Spirit would say, "Girl, you need to fix this."

Going back to the night at the airport, eventually, I fell asleep, even with the lady on the phone talking loudly, and I awoke just in time to prepare to get my ticket. As I was organizing my bags to go to the ticket counter, God told me to write "John 3:16" on a piece of paper and give one to each of the three people who had spent the night near me. He also instructed me to write "You are loved" at the top and then the scripture. Afterwards, I safely boarded the plane and went home.

However, when I got home, I felt physically and mentally exhausted as a result of doing a quick turn-around trip and sleeping at the airport. As I reflected on the trip, I began to become infuriated because I felt like I had wasted money on airline tickets. The thoughts in my head ranged from *You aren't hearing from God, to You are going to be penniless if you keep thinking you hear from God, and You can't possibly hear from God. You are such a bad businesswoman.* Even my son gave me the blues. He chimed in, adding to the negative thoughts I was having by telling me that I did not have good business sense. He stated that I wasn't dumb, but that I acted "like a blonde". If you are blonde, I apologize, but those were his words. Now, add his words to my thoughts! I was really in the dumps trying to figure things out, and looking at the financial loss did not help at all.

After sleeping nearly the entire day, I woke up the following morning. I didn't even get to put my timer on to spend time with the Holy Spirit, because God immediately said, "Glad you are up. Now, tell me: how can you put a value on the lives of the three people who you reminded that I loved them?" *Bam!* I was slapped in the face with the truth of God. There is no way I could say that anyone's life was worth the money I spent on plane tickets. How selfish of me! Just like Isaac, I thought only of myself (see Genesis 26: 7-10). I did not ask God what His plan for the trip was, I only asked God if I should go and seek that opportunity. The opportunity I had planned turned out to be completely different from what God had planned.

"Stop being selfish!" – I hear you, Father.

CHAPTER 10

Stop Playing Dress-Up

When living in a world that promotes being selfish, we tend to believe that it is okay to think of only ourselves (see 2 Timothy 3:2). We act as if the other person has no choices. As a result, we make choices for them based on our selfishness. For this reason, we have hurt many innocent children who did not deserve to be abandoned. More specifically, I would like to speak against a law that I once supported and participated in. There is no doubt in my spirit that this law was implemented to carry out Satan's plan to get God's children to participate in his schemes (see John 8:44). This law permits us to kill the innocent and act like Herod, who killed all the boys for his own selfish reasons (Matthew 2:16-18). Many believers have participated in similar acts, causing them to feel guilty, use drugs, commit suicide, or engage in other acts to help relieve them of the agony associated with abortion. Let me be frank with everyone. Abortion is a murderous act.

As a society, under this law, we have killed many innocent children and caused them not to have the opportunity to live and serve God. We strip them of the gift of life that God had given them. Before you become overly depressed or super holy, I suggest you remember that we all have sinned and fallen short of His glory, but the beauty of the story is the ending: when we repent, God forgives us. So, if you have had an abortion, please keep reading, because this will bless you and help you with your healing process. If you have not had an abortion, keep reading as well. This will help provide insight so that you can understand that God sees all our ways as sinful when they are not righteous. With this in mind, we are to encourage each other and be healed instead of condemning each other and hurting, according to James 5:16.

I know you are probably thinking, *Well, it was an abortion, and it was legal, so I was within my legal rights to abort the child.* Yes, according to man's law, it is legal to have an abortion. However, God does not see it as a right that we should act upon because it is not righteous. As believers, we are the righteousness of God. Therefore, we do not act like the world, and we do not engage in laws that defy God as the authority, and by committing murder, we are breaking our Father's laws.

God has shown me that no matter how I tried to justify my reasons when I chose to have an abortion, I still committed murder. I took the life of a child – correction, children – who had no part in my selfish decision to have sex without being married and to abort the life that was in me. If you have had an abortion and you think it was okay, let me make this clear to you that until you accept the truth about what you did, you will struggle with receiving forgiveness, and if you still are convinced that your ways were not selfish, please continue to read. I am sure that if you would take a moment to think about why you chose to have an abortion, at no point did you think about the child's right to live, nor did you consult God.

If you don't think having an abortion demonstrates a selfish behavior, please ask God to give you insight. No, He will not judge you, and I am not judging you either. Who am I to judge anyone or anything? I just want you to be completely healed and free of the guilt that burdens us after we have an abortion. Our Father will not tell you that you are a horrible person, but He will teach you to be compassionate towards others who have had an abortion or those who do not understand why you chose to have an abortion. Your heavenly Father will forgive you because He loves you. That is the truth of all things that you will ever read and know. Your Father loves you, and He cares about you.

There is nothing you can do that will cause Him not to love you. He will forgive you when you ask for forgiveness. He will comfort you as you begin to embrace the love He has for you. If you think I didn't have an initial struggle to accept His forgiveness, think again. I am a preacher's daughter who grew up in the church. I had felt the presence of the Holy Spirit in my life, so I knew God was real, but when I was living my life chasing and doing what I wanted, I forgot about who God was. I started living life *my* way and doing what I wanted to do. While living foolishly, I got pregnant and aborted the children. Yes, plural, meaning more than one.

Now, try living with this daily. The demonic spirits played with my thoughts after having my third abortion. That is right – three abortions, and I still am forgiven. No one can make me feel guilty because my Father has forgiven me. He does not condemn. Thoughts of condemnation and destruction come from those demonic spirits who were silent when I went through the ordeal. They knew that I was creating a way for them to hold me in bondage. Someone reading this might say that I was having an abortion as a way of birth control. Yep, you are right – I was controlling the births that I did not want to allow to exist in this world. No, I did not have them back to back, and I am not trying to justify my ways. I want you to know that these decisions happened because I only thought of myself. I did not ask for help, and I did not speak to my parents about my decision. Did I regret them afterwards? *Yes*, I did.

I regretted my last abortion the most. It was clearly my decision – my own selfish decision, because if I had told the father, he would have been okay if we had kept the child. However, I made him think that I did not want the child because of my fear of him telling me he did not want to have a child. Where did I get this from? It was from overloaded baggage that I had brought with me from my previous relationship, and because I didn't talk to the father of the child about my true feelings or express to him that I wanted the child, I aborted him.

In the past, sharing this truth would have over-whelmed me with grief, but I know that my God has forgiven me. I am no longer ashamed of my past. I am healed from my past and I want to share it to help heal others. Boldly, I share my ungodly decisions with others to help save them. I want the world to know that I am a sinner who is truly redeemed by Jesus, as I know the bruises that He endured were for me so that I could be seen as righteous (see Isaiah 53:5). Being righteous is our gift (see Romans 5:17). We cannot earn righteous-ness because Jesus freely gave this gift to us so that we could live and be loved. Accept Jesus' gift.

God has healed me and delivered me from the things I used to do. Now, I make sure that my only living son knows that if he gets a girl pregnant, an abortion is not an option, because if he dabbles in sin and conceives a child, the child is his and he has no authority to take that child's life. I hope he gets the message.

Many people who have not had an abortion do not know the impact that this decision can have on the mother later on in life. We must know that an abortion leaves a way for demonic spirits to come and make strong suggestions about who we are and why God does not love us. Well, I always like to go to my power-up book – the Bible. Please don't think that the Bible was without abortion. The true definition of an abortion is a child killed with the mother's participation, let's be honest.

Now, for those of us who still do not recall seeing an abortion in the Bible, consider this revelation in 1 Kings 3:19. In this passage, a baby died at the hand of its mother, who was so full of selfishness that she also wanted to kill her prostitute colleague's baby too. Do you know who I am talking about? I am referring to the two prostitutes who went to King Solomon. The first prostitute complained because the second prostitute had taken her child and was claiming him as her own. The second prostitute knew that she had murdered or aborted her child, but she was okay with causing pain to the first prostitute because she did not want to deal with what she had done.

You see, when you have an abortion, the first thing that comes at you is guilt. You try to cover up what you did. You do not tell anyone else about your life choice, and you really don't want to deal with the pain of your loss because it hurts. Like the second prostitute, you might even lie to cover up what you did. Notice too that they were both prostitutes, meaning their children were born out of wedlock. That was me. I had the babies out of wedlock, so the abortions were out of wedlock too. Like these two women, I was engaging in sexual immorality, as I was enjoying sex and having a time of my life – or at least I thought I was having a grand time. It was all fake. The whole relationship was a fake, including the guy, who was later revealed to be a con artist who easily manipulated me because I really did not know who I was in God. Who I was, for the most part, reflected a very selfish person who was not connected to God, so I was blind and did not see his abuse. I was too tied up in how good he made me feel sexually. Having sex without being committed to God leads to challenging encounters with demonic spirits. However, when we implement God's plan for family and sex, we put His will first in our lives.

As obedient children to God, we must not have sex until we are married. If I had adhered to this principle, that would have solved my decision and the two prostitutes' decisions, but like the prostitutes, I was having sex for trinkets. The prostitutes were wise – when an issue arose, they knew who to go to. They went straight to King Solomon for help. Why did they go to him? They went because King Solomon was a man of authority who made just decisions with the wisdom of God. When we have issues, who we go to for help impacts the outcome of the situation. As believers, we need to identify our problems and present them to God. Going to our Father when we have issues can save us a lot of time. It can give us an opportunity to make changes and overcome dangerous acts before things get out of control. Had I listened to my parents or even sought God, I would not have gotten an abortion, because doing wrong and trying to cover it up leads to a battle that creates disruption in our lives. Repent and ask God for forgiveness, and I mean *really* repent by listening to the Holy Spirit and stop committing the same sin. This means to stop acting and doing things that deny God's presence in our lives. Once we repent, God will have mercy on us. The way we repent is by changing our sinful ways. We are not to condemn ourselves, but we are to acknowledge the presence of God in our lives.

If sex is your sin that you get entangled with, stop having sex. If lying is your sin, stop lying. If stealing is your sin, stop stealing. I believe that the reason I suffered financially was because of my sin of aborting my children. Better yet, it was connected to the root of my sin, which was sex. I did not want to deal with the children who were a result of my choices. My excuse of lacking finances to support them or lacking time to take care of them because they would have interrupted my life was more than I wanted to deal with. I am grateful for God having mercy on me and for forgiving my sin. I know that since I have openly confessed my sins and asked God to forgive me, I am forgiven. Therefore, I can proceed with life and be delivered from the curse of poverty, bondage, imperfection, and every other form of need. I am free. Thank You, Jesus, for redeeming me, and Father, thank You for being so patient and loving me as a sinner. Please do not read any of this passage and think that you are not forgiven, because you are. Sure, you will sin again, but you will become more conscious of your ways, which will mold you into being who God wants you to be.

Let me get back to the two prostitutes who went to King Solomon. As I said, even though their lives were not pleasing to God, they recognized when they needed to seek someone in authority for help. The first prostitute pleaded her case to King Solomon. Likewise, we need to go to God to plead our case and ask for His divine intervention in our lives. We need to ask our Father to have mercy on us. This requires us to be like the prostitute and recognize who is in authority, tell the truth about our sins and transgressions, identify our part in the situation, and take responsibility for our actions by openly confessing the truth to our Father. Just as sure as Solomon heard the two prostitutes, our Lord will hear us.

Did you notice what the second prostitute did? She refused to recognize her wrongdoing, which was that she killed her son. Instead of mourning his death and taking the responsibility, she tried to cover up her sin. How many times have we done wrong and tried to cover it up? Many of us have tried to cover it to prevent our friends and family from knowing the truth. My parents never knew of my decision to have several abortions. Why did I not tell them? I knew they would not approve of my behavior. They would have encouraged me to have the babies, but because I was selfish, I kept it a secret like the second prostitute. It is important to be mindful when we are in distress or dealing with a bad situation in life; we need to be careful of who we let give us advice or who tries to persuade us against what we know is true.

We need discernment to help us know who is providing guidance that leads to doing what God directs us to do. When we are in an emotional situation, people can give us pretty good reasons that *sound* good, but do not support what is truly right to do. This is evident when we reflect on the second prostitute, as she must have been convincing to King Solomon because he was not even sure who was telling the truth. However, because of the spirit of wisdom that God had given him, King Solomon was able to identify the truth. Similarly, God recognizes our hearts and knows when we are honestly seeking Him to change from our ways that pleases our flesh to wanting to know who He is. Therefore, seek Him for guidance and follow His plan for your life, because even though it might seem to be an inconvenience for that moment, it will have a better outcome.

Don't keep lying like the second prostitute.

Unfortunately, the second prostitute didn't even know when to stop lying. She wanted to keep her story going at the cost of things that did not belong to her. She was willing to split the child in half, which she knew would have meant the child would die. However, her selfishness revealed the truth. Allow your selfishness to reveal your truth. If you had an abortion, tell God the truth about your decision. He will hear you, and you will know that He has been waiting a long time to have this conversation of love with you.

Stop regretting your decision and start living in love. Trash the guilt and live in purpose. Don't hide your truth, but tell it, so that others won't make the same mistake. Tell your truth so that others can see your flaws of love. Yes, our flaws of love, meaning we made errors, but God sees them as opportunities to show His love. His love is revealed in the process of your healing and will set you free from the bondage that held you from moving forward in life. Stop living a life full of lies that are infesting your mind daily. These lies will only make you feel like you are in bondage, unloved, and unforgiven. Your honesty will win God's approval, unlike lies. As we know, God truly detests lies because they are the greatest trick that Satan uses against us (see John 8:44). Satan speaks lies to us daily because he is the father of lies, so we need to learn to fend him off with the Word of God. He wants to tell us that our Father does not love us because we had an abortion.

When these thoughts come to you, tell him to shut up. Then, find a scripture, and when the dark or demonic spirits try to tell you who you are, remind them of who God says you are. Find any passage about love – read it, because this is the message your heavenly Father wants to send to you every day of your life. He wants to tell you that He loves you and you are not the same person anymore. You are truly redeemed and cared for. Trust what God tells you, not the manipulating, lying Satan. Admit the truth: ask for forgiveness and no one will have the right to take what belongs to you, which is your gift of salvation from Jesus.

Say this prayer and know that you are forgiven:

Dear loving Father, You are almighty and all powerful. No one can compare to You because You are long-suffering, forgiving, caring, and merciful. You are the only wise God. Search my heart today and find the compassion I have for You. I ask You to search me to help me identify the areas in which I need to repent. I know that I have sinned and that I will sin again, but I choose not to sin, knowing that my ways are not Your ways. I ask You, Father, to have mercy on me and to forgive me so that I can live as You direct me to live. Let the Holy Spirit speak to me and give me guidance so that I might learn of Your ways. I yearn to know You, and I will read Your Word daily so that I can know more about who You are and how to be in the right relationship with You. Hallelujah, almighty God! You have the power to let it be so. Therefore, I ask You to forgive me of my sins and have mercy on me, Father, as I walk in Your love. In Jesus' name I pray, amen.

From this day forward, let us live as the righteous children of God. Let us do as God commands us by being dead to sin and checking each word against the scripture. Let us see our Father's way and how we are not serving Him so that we can learn more of the truth. By turning to God, we will receive our crown of righteousness and enjoy a victorious life in this world. Let us recognize that even though we are within our earthly rights, we must not do things that deny God. Let us be like Shadrack, Meshack and Abednego by refusing to follow laws that place themselves above our sovereign

God. Most importantly, let us commit to receiving our Father's forgiveness and His love for us.

CHAPTER 11

Gathering the Pieces

Earlier, I shared how I was in bondage to sex and how I was able to receive my healing from guilt and shame. I would like to elaborate more on how God has helped me through this process by allowing me to see His love. First, I had to acknowledge how I had allowed prostitution in my life through my selfish ways. Like some of you, I gladly proclaimed my success in collecting pay for sex. With wealthy patrons, male partners, or however you want to describe them, I established a good business plan that allowed me to enjoy many trinkets in exchange for sexual pleasures.

Do you think that you haven't prostituted yourself? Really? That's good to know, but if you have ever slept with a man in exchange for a meal, a bill payment, a trip, prestige, or sexual pleasure, you engaged in prostitution. This downplay of reality is only the beginning of how we justify our ways so that they are more pleasing to ourselves and friends than our King. However, it's all good, because no matter what you exchanged your body for, there is victory in knowing that you have a purpose that is based on your past. When you connect to the power of the Holy Spirit and renew your mind to think as God thinks, you will fulfill your purpose.

Your purpose is hidden in your past skills, sins or challenges. Do you recall Rahab? Rahab was a prostitute, and she is in our Father's love letter to us! As a matter of a fact, she is also in the lineage of Jesus (see Matthew 1:5). With her presence, along with that of Bathsheba, who is also in the lineage of Jesus (see Matthew 1:6), I feel that God was reassuring us that He loves us and wants to use us to be a part of His kingdom. He is saying that He is so forgiving that He permitted a former prostitute and a woman who committed adultery to be part of His Son's bloodline. So, do not let Satan or his demonic spirits tell you that your Lord does not love you, because He does. Our Father is clearly saying that He loves us and that He wants to be a part of our lives. He does not care about our past, and He only cares about our future. From this moment forward, live knowing the truth of how much you are loved. Don't let your past prevent you from living a life full of goodness and mercy that is constantly following you to cover all your sins and to give you strength to endure.

If you are like me, many of us have lived a life in which we did not show any kind of behavior of repentance because we really *enjoyed* living for Satan—and I mean we enjoyed our sinful life. Whatever your sin of choice was, it was yours, whether it was sexual immorality, lying, witchcraft, divination, or any combination of sinful acts that God detests. It was a sin that you chose to continue to commit. We have spent time engaged in our sinful ways, and we even imagined or prepared the event in our minds prior to participating in it. Just like we spent time preparing for these sinful acts that we committed, we also need to spend time with our Lord. As we spend time with Him, we will be ecstatic and overjoyed with His love for us.

When we peek into Rahab's life, we can see that our Father has shown us that when we trust Him and stop serving Satan, our past will lead to helping others grow to know Christ, which will give them access to the kingdom of God. Perhaps we think that we are not serving Satan because we are not a member of a satanic group. However, in Matthew 6:24, the distinction is clearly made. We will either serve one or hate the other. Through our actions, we demonstrate who we serve even though we go to church on Sunday and Bible study during the week. It is what we do when we are not under the watchful eye of other believers that tells the truth of who we are. It is time for us to acknowledge our Father as the one and only true God. Our Lord has given us the opportunity to choose what we will do and how we will live as we make decisions on earth that will influence our eternal choice.

Our Father has been watching us every day of our life and has been waiting for the day to have us realize how much He cares for us. As obedient children of God, we need to repent and spend designated time with Him. Repenting does not mean having a feeling of remorse and feeling sorrowful as if we are feeling some form of wretchedness. Repenting means that we change our way of thinking. Every day, we seek to think on things that are noble, lovely, admirable, excellent, and praiseworthy (see Philippians 4:8). God is not holding our sins against us (see Hebrews 8:12).

As we willingly come to Him to accept that He loves us and that He is not out to punish us with an unforgiving heart, we will see our purpose as one with authority on earth who is loved. Now, we will endure a season in which we must be prayerful and trust God through challenging situations, but trusting God through the process will allow Him to see our hearts, and if He had mercy on King Ahab, then surely He will have mercy on us. Trusting God can cause our lives to change drastically. For this reason, God warns us to seek the kingdom of God. Seeking the kingdom of God allows us to connect with the Holy Spirit and renew our minds to be like our Lord's. There will be moments when you will notice that the things that used to bring you joy no longer satisfy you. Why? You have found a new purpose in your Father. You crave to serve Him as your Lord, and you seek daily His way for your life (see Phillippians 3:13-14).

We must remember that as we live our lives, we will be in battle with the spirits of darkness. They will continuously try to bind us in our minds to keep us from trusting in what our Lord says. They want to keep us enslaved to the way they think and conduct things on earth. Just like Satan wanted to bind Jesus in death clothing, which was a traditional garment, he also wants to keep you in bondage. What these spirits realize is that once you are delivered, you will have a powerful impact on the lives of others. You just need to escape his captivity by repenting to our Lord and following His plan for your life. When you receive your redemption from the blood of Jesus, you will be free to live the planned life that our Father has for you. Yes, Jesus is our escape clause so that we can be seen as righteous. Once you escape, you can share your story to help others get free.

Our Father is asking, "Will you accept My love, repent by changing your thinking, and work with Me to bring others to know Me? Are you ready to make the change today?" Once you make the change, there will be opportunities for you to fall back into the way you used to do things. When you are faced with the opportunity, know that it was destined to happen and that the spirits want to pull you back into their death clause. We must become more aware of the One who can judge us in the end. Your eternity is at stake, and if you are like me, you have accepted the love of your Father and you do not want to create distance in your relationship with Him. Our Father loves us, and He does not want to punish us for our past. He wants us to go forward, being a witness for Him while enjoying His favor on our lives.

This truth is evident when we look at Rahab. I love Rahab because despite her past, she knew when to stop being manipulated by the spirit of sexual immorality. She exhibited her faith in God when she first let the two spies into her home. She might not have had a relationship with God, but she had heard about how He had given the Israelites victory. She knew that defeat was coming, and she wanted to change her position in the outcome. Only our Lord can set up rescue through unforeseen means.

When our Lord sends His rescue to you, it should signify that He is always in the process of making things work out for us. Our Father shows us that He cares for us by allowing us to see how Rahab implements her faith and goes on to be a part of our Savior's bloodline. Therefore, no matter what you have encountered or done in the past, know that your Father cares about you, not the situation. You are His treasured child. I often look at myself as being like the prodigal son. I know that I must have heard my father preach this sermon over a dozen times, but it was not until I dealt with my need to truly change that I realized the value of this story. The love letter from our Father is full of examples that demonstrate His care for us. We just must stop giving the spirits of darkness the power to beat us up with our past mistakes, because those mistakes can lead to victory for others.

Let's look at Rahab's skills and gifts. It is very important to pay attention to how she used them to secure safety for herself and her family. Rahab was a businesswoman – whether you want to accept prostitution as a business or not, it is. In her line of work, she knew how to get what she needed for her family to survive. She was not selfish, nor did she lack knowledge of God, as she had paid close attention to what God had done for His people. It is also important to recognize that Rahab was a successful prostitute because she had her own place, so that means she made good money as an entrepreneur. She was not living with a man who took care of her, but she had used what she possessed to fund her family's lifestyle.

Now look, don't go thinking that I am saying this is a profession that we should indulge in. I am sure that some of us have acted in the same manner as Rahab in order to get what we want. As I have said earlier, I was a prostitute because I collected the things that I needed from the men I encountered, and if they did not pay, they got left behind. I don't care if you think prostitution is the norm, it is not the God-approved way of interacting with men. It is a manipulative way to exchange time and sex for goods. If you are having sex with a man that is not your husband, could it be that you are prostituting yourself? Either way, you are acting against what God has said. We are not to commit adultery or fornication.

Let's get back to Rahab. She did not suffer or lack because she was able to take care of the spies. I am sure she fed them, and they were not hungry while waiting on the roof of her home. Rahab was a woman who recognized whose side to be on. She knew how to bargain with men to get what she wanted. That means she possessed a special way of talking to men, which would explain her ability to be a successful prostitute who had a nice home with a window on the wall. In other words, Rahab's place came with a view of the countryside. Her home wasn't small either, because Rahab was able to get her entire family and her family's servants in her home. Her wealth shows her gift of persuasion and her ability to negotiate.

Rahab had to be very good with the services she provided, and she knew how to talk to men, as she was able to get the soldiers to believe her with ease when she told them that the spies had left. God used Rahab's skills to protect the Israelite spies. Rahab must have been believable when the guards came to her home to get the spies. She was convincingly ready with her lying response, as I am sure she had a lot of practice lying while working as a prostitute. When engaging with the soldiers, Rahab used the lying spirit to save the lives of the Israelite spies (she didn't *really* lie, because technically they were not in her home, they were on the roof). The fact is, she intervened to preserve the lives of the two spies. Rahab was also a good negotiator. She negotiated protection for herself, her family, and those who were part of her family's household. In other words, Rahab pleaded for the lives of her family and their servants because she respected the power of our Lord.

Negotiation is a good skill to have. I am sure this was another skill she had perfected as a prostitute, as she had to negotiate with men to get them to pay for her services. Had Rahab negotiated with the guards who came to get the two Israelite spies, this would have resulted in a very different outcome. Rahab's life, along with her family's lives, would not have been spared, because I am sure God would have used someone else to take care of the spies. Now, we also know that Rahab

recognized that God was powerful, and she acknowl-
edged how God had shown He was with the Israelites.
She knew that God was a one-of-a-kind, almighty God
and there was no one like Him. Rahab wanted to be on
the winning team. As a result, she kept her mouth shut,
tied a scarf around her window, and was saved. Rahab
knew when to change so that she could be used by God.
Do you know when to cease your sinful life and recognize God as the sovereign King?

Like Rahab, I spent days negotiating with men to get
what I wanted. If I did not get the results that I wanted
from one man, then my time was spent with a different
man who *did* give me what I wanted. My characteristic
traits were that of a prostitute, although in our society
I was not looked upon as a prostitute by my associates.
We would discuss the benefits of the men we had in our
lives while in these relationships. My life choices even
included bragging about my behavior. I am so glad that
when the day came for me to recognize that I was making choices that were not a representation of an heir
of God's kingdom, I repented and discontinued living
as if sexual immorality was my god. When faced with
my reality, I started making changes because I knew I
was only going to fall deeper under the submission of
Satan when God was calling me to transform. I packed
my things and planned my escape before the walls of
Jericho started tumbling down. In other words, before

the only God-fearing part of me left disintegrated into complete ashes, I stopped and listened to the Holy Spirit so that He could point me in the direction that He wanted me to go. Listening to the Holy Spirit was a big change for me because I had spent years doing things my way.

The truth of my life is that I know I am not able to make changes without my Father's intervention. Daily, He directs me and speaks to me through the Holy Spirit so that I can work on becoming more like one who knows the truth of who I am. I know that God has a purpose for my life, just like He did for Rahab, and I want to be known for helping to build the kingdom of God. God's kingdom is all that matters. I know and understand this now. Because I accept that I am directed to live a certain way and I do not think I am so righteous, I can tell you the truth about my encounters so that I can encourage you to see the truth of who you are and who God wants you to be. Whatever your situation, whatever you have done – you are not those things. You have the right to live as God has promised you to live. Do not become overwhelmed with your past, as there are many people who have overcome challenges, and you can, too (see Romans 4:7). Keep trusting and growing to know who you are. Identify the skills that you have, identify the challenges our Lord has helped you overcome, and embrace your Father's forgiveness.

Satan will always try to challenge who you are once you start living your life with your Father in your heart and mind, but know that your Father loves you. His love for you will comfort you when you feel lonely, unlovable, and distraught. Find a way to allow your Lord's truth to get into your heart. Sometimes, I have to listen to messages on YouTube, gospel music, or the Bible when I feel as if I am in a mental battle. You will have to do this whenever you feel overwhelmed so that you can transform your mind. Transforming your mind requires daily action from us to make sure our Father's truth about us is in the forefront of our minds.

We must keep studying the Word to know the meaning of what He says. The Bible is very powerful, and it has a message that will help you. The messages will help you identify your purpose – you just need to be willing to listen to the Holy Spirit when He speaks and take action towards your healing journey. Use your past to help others as they struggle with the same issue. If you suffered from drug addiction, was there a time when you persuaded a drug dealer to give you the product on credit? That is a skill of persuasion. Some of us have great negotiating skills that we can use for good. Use your talents to save others. It will make your struggles seem worth your time and journey. Help save someone else who desperately needs your loving understanding in order to overcome.

CHAPTER 12

Stop Tripping and Start Snipping

Moving forward can be a big challenge when we are desperately trying to get from a situation in which we felt unforgivable to knowing that we are forgiven. Our minds start tripping when Satan tells us how horrible we are and how we are so stupid. These thoughts require us to snip away at the lies of unforgiveness. To get there, I had to welcome this truth: that I know my God loves me. You can move forward knowing that He loves you too. He cared so much for our well-being that He left his plans and road map for us to follow. All of His commandments and desires for us are written in the Bible, and we can put our entire existence and future into God's hand while finding what He instructs us to do in His love letter to us.

Look, if it was not for the Bible, we would have no way to repel the enemy: Satan. We would have little to go on in believing the existence of God, but with the

Word that God has given us, we can overcome every encounter in our life. The Bible was provided to us for a reason, and that reason is so that we can live victorious in God's name. We can live knowing that God loves us and that He will forgive us of our sins. We can live knowing that He is not in heaven with a red marker, ready to identify every area in our lives that we have messed up or made a mistake. That is not who God is, and if you ever doubt this, read your Bible. See how forgiving He was, even to Ahab. See how forgiving He was to the children of Israel who witnessed the miraculous hand of God.

Our Father is so patient, loving, and kind. He wants us to live life knowing that we can trust Him to mercifully intervene in our lives with grace. His loving hand covers and protects us from dangers. He sees the good in us because we are His children. Like any loving father, He wants the best for us while we live on earth, and He wants us to spend eternity in His presence. To make sure that we had insight of His plans for our life, He commanded men to write the Bible. It is the best survivor book that you and I have. I can go to it and find scriptures to help me live daily, knowing of God's grace and love for me; so can you.

I know there are times when I am in the thick of spiritual warfare and I will begin to feel heaviness accompanied with thoughts of not being good enough.

These thoughts come as small suggestions, but I often end up having a full-blown conversation with myself in my head. I know this happens more frequently when I am dealing with situations that are not going as I thought they should. These thoughts are reminders that demonic spirits are out to destroy me with a vengeance. However, I do not engage in war without knowing the truth.

Many battles occur in my thoughts. I know that there are specific weapons to use during the war. If you are like me, there have been times when you play out an entire scenario in your head based on a few facts and a lot of speculations. As a result, fear, anxiety, or anger creeps in and sets up camp. These spirits get a hold of your thought pattern to prevent you from going with what God says, which is to not worry or fret because He has given us the spirit of power, the spirit of love, and the spirit of self-discipline (see 2 Timothy 1:7). Any spirit that contradicts these gifts from God is not from Him. Snatch back your mind and transform it to where you know that your Father loves you. He cares for you and His plans for your life do not create or illustrate anything but love. "'For I know the plans I have for you,' declares the Lord, 'plans to prosper you and not to harm you, plans to give you hope and a future'" (Jeremiah 29:11, NIV).

This is the plan that Satan does not want you to complete. This is the plan that says to the world that our Father is real and He is the one who provides for us, not man. When we search the Word of our Lord and allow Him to reveal what is true to us, it will have a greater impact on the world than our mere plans do. It is in our love for our Lord that we show we trust Him to do what is best for us. Having faith demonstrates our love for Him. You cannot have faith in Him if you do not love Him. Loving our Lord opens doors to the beauty of knowing Him as our personal Father. Knowing Him to be caring, compassionate, and willing to help us allows us to see His love for us. We must be willing to know Him – knowing Him through His love for us. By doing this, we are relieved from any form of burden that is placed on us because of our sins. Are you ready to run into your Father's arms and let Him love you? He has been waiting.

I wish I could tell you that once you run to your Father and allow Him to love you that you will never encounter any issues. I cannot. Well, I suppose I could, but it would be a lie. However, I can tell you that once you accept His love and allow Him to love you, you will have better insight on why things are happening and you will be forever comforted with His love, even when you make a mistake. Remember, we are forever in a battle until we are called home to be with Him. Perhaps you are thinking, *Then why doesn't He just call me home? I am tired and ready to go.* If you are having suicidal thoughts, please seek help. Do not feel ashamed or unworthy. Seek the help you need so that you can be healed.

If you wonder why He allows us to go through challenges, the answer is simple one – we belong to Him and He has a far greater purpose for your life. Because He is our creator, His plans overrule our plans. Do you remember when you were in school and you planned to sit quietly in class without answering any questions because you only cared about being counted as present? In life, you try to implement this same strategy. You didn't have that option then and you don't have it now when it comes to completing what our Father wants us to do. Embrace this truth: if you were not so vital to His plan, then Satan would not be trying so hard to destroy you. You are an important part of the message from God. So, whatever God is instructing you to do, know that He has told you this for a reason. He wants you to transform your thinking and get ready to fight the good fight of faith, armed with His Word.

Many times, I have made mistakes, but I am learning one key thing: when I make a mistake, I should ask for forgiveness as soon as it is brought to my attention. I know that once I repent, God forgives me. I also know that the enemy wants to use these mistakes against me with thoughts of disobedience and unforgiveness. He wants to tell me that my Lord is going to punish me for being so disobedient, and he is quick to say that I am not forgiven. Recognize Satan's pattern. He uses the same old tricks and mind games against us to keep us in bondage. Remember, he has an agenda, which is to keep you from knowing who you are. His plan is everything that is the opposite of what your Father says and does. Therefore, as soon as you recognize his tactic, remind yourself of your Lord's love for you. Fight the battle and move forward to conquer in God's grace.

While in battle, I have learned to follow Jesus' pattern. When Satan tried to get into Jesus' mind with words to create doubt, Jesus quoted scriptures. When Satan tried to tempt Jesus with what he knew was not the right way to get what God promised Him, he quoted a scripture. When Satan tried to appeal to Jesus' flesh, he quoted a scripture. That is it. To quote a scripture, you need to know them. To know them, you need to read the Bible. When we read the Bible, God will connect you to His Word because of the Holy Spirit in you.

You might not even know where the scripture really is in the Bible when you first start out, but just believe what God says. God says that He loves you (see John 3:16). God says that you are forgiven (see Colossians 3:13). God says that you are healed (see 1 Peter 2:24). Do not just take Satan's suggestions and let them manifest in your mind. God wants to save you. God cares about you. If He did not, He would not have left this equipment for us to have access to when battling the enemy. I do not have to get angry or fret. I do not have to look at my current life's situation and say, "This is how it is going to be forever." I have been there mentally, spiritually, and physically before; the only difference is that I had a plan that I thought created success. I did not see God's hand in it, nor did I see it as Him saving me again, so the results were the same, because time and time again when He saved me from a situation, I reverted to my way of doing and set off without God. I failed, all because I relied solely on me and what I had done to be able to enjoy my current state of success. I did not give glory to God for saving me.

At first, when I realized how much I had lost due to my connection with scrupulous people, I began to blame them. I was angry because they did not do as they had promised, but during my anger, God told me that I had not done as He expected of me. I had not kept my promise to Him. I was enjoying the fruit of my labor without giving Him His tithe. I had robbed Him once again, and I had walked out with my inheritance, living amongst prostitutes like the prodigal son. Yes, that is how I chose to live, but when I realized that I was in the hog pit about to eat slop, I came to myself. I heard the voice of God and I changed. Praise the Lord for His mercy, as it allowed me to be able to share my story with you today. I am not overwhelmed with depression or anxiety. God keeps providing daily manna, and I receive it. I am grateful when He brings it, and I say, "Thank You," because He remembers my needs and honors His word. You see, I never would have gotten to this point if I had not admitted my sin and made a commitment to follow God.

I made it publicly known that I loved sex and was using drugs, but that is no longer my lifestyle. I knew there was hope for me. I know that God has a plan for me because He forgave Peter, who doubted Him even though he walked with Jesus. I know He forgives me and He also forgives you. How forgiving God is can be found everywhere in the Bible. Both Jesus and God have shown how they love us more than they hate the sins that we commit. For this reason, they are more willing to forgive. As a matter of a fact, Jesus has encountered the challenges that we have faced, so He speaks up for us to our Father. Jesus is a great example of God's love and it is evident in His actions towards those whom He loved.

You see, Jesus loved Peter even though He knew Peter was going to deny Him. Jesus still washed Peter's feet while knowing that His disciple would one day pretend that he had no idea who He was (see John 13:1-17 and Luke 22:54-62). This example shows us a multitude of things. It shows us that we should be forgiving even when a person has mistreated us. It shows that we are still loved when we make mistakes. It shows that even though we love our Lord, Jesus, and the Holy Spirit, we still will deny them by our words and actions even though they know this, and it is okay. It's okay because it's real love. It is not the type of superficial and temperamental love that we share with each other. So, when we are prompted by Satan to feel unloved, we need to quickly address this thought with the Word.

First, we are made in God's image (see Genesis 1:27), and God loves us so much that He sent Jesus to suffer for us (see John 15:13). Jesus came, knowing He was going to be treated badly, but His compassion for us exemplifies the depth of God's love for us. Jesus' willingness to prove the depths of God's love and His trust in Him is evident because Jesus knew His reward would be to save us so that we could enjoy life knowing how much He cares for us. So, stop feeling bad for yourself. Get out your Bible and read the Word that heals us all. God's love letter tells the truth about why we are created and it shows us repeatedly through the lives of others in the scriptures that our Father is forgiving.

If you are like me, or shall I say were like me, Bible reading was limited to church scriptures on Sunday morning, but not anymore. Reading my Bible daily for the purpose of getting to know God and how much He cares about me is part of my life. I also spend time praying for everything. When I cannot figure things out, I pause to hear from God. He is the only one I aim to glorify daily. By glorifying Him and following His way, I know that I receive His peace and instruction. If I make a mistake and talk over someone, lie, or even say what He told me to not say, I repent immediately. I do not want to be bound by my old ways. I want to live a free life with the promise of my Lord's intervention. He is my very present help in the time of need (see Psalm 46:1).

CHAPTER 13

Start Ditching and Stitching

Ditch that thought of doubt. I know I have said this before, but I want to say it again because it is very important to ditch it. Ditch it immediately. Do not play out that scenario in your head, because you do not have room for it in your mind. Ditch the feeling of unworthiness – it does not belong in your head space. Start stitching into every seam of your mind that your Father loves you and has left you the greatest love letter ever. Read it. Be healed and know that everything that contradicts our love letter is a lie. Live knowing you are loved and look for your love message in the Word. I did. It helped me to know how much my Lord loves me.

I know my Lord provided His Word to help me heal during this time in which demonic spirits try to fill me with guilt. I know that God has forgiven me and that He loves me, so I wait patiently while planting seeds of hope and faith. I know that the opportunity to advance

in business is waiting on me as long as I listen to the
Holy Spirit and trust God's plan. I know that He keeps
giving me invention ideas because He was a creator, so
I am designed to create too. I keep doing what God says
by planting seeds and following His way. I know I will
be okay. I am not going to stress. I am not going to worry. I am putting things totally in God's hand, because if
God didn't care for a person like me, there would not be
information about a woman named Bathsheba in the
Bible.

Let me refresh your memory regarding my friend
Bathsheba. Bathsheba was married to Uriah. Uriah was
in the military and served as a loyal soldier. Now, Bathsheba was extremely good looking. King David saw her
taking a bath while he was on the rooftop, and just from
a simple glimpse of Bathsheba, he wanted to have her.
So, like most men, he sought to find out who this beautiful woman was, and even though he found out that
she was married to someone else, he still craved her.
Since Bathsheba loved men who were in authority and
who were brave, she willingly went to kick it with David. I do not doubt that she had even planned or dreamt
of being with him prior to him asking her. They had
a night full of sexual pleasure, and Bam! She became
pregnant with a baby boy.

Now, you know that Bathsheba knew when she con-
ceived that the baby was not her husband's child be-

cause she had just come off her menstrual cycle, her husband was at war, and the only man that she had been with was King David. That is a word for someone right there. You slept with that man one time, and you got pregnant. You really had not planned on things turning out this way. As a matter of a fact, it was supposed to have been a one-night stand. Maybe you felt angry, emotional, sex-deprived, or lonely (it really does not matter at this point), so you decided in your mind to have sex with someone who was not yours.

Now, for the woman who says, "No, he was my man and we have been together for years." Let me tell you this: if you are not married to him, he does not belong to you, regardless if you were the only one he was seeing, because as believers, we are not our own. We belong to God, and He commands us to not engage in sexual immorality. Our Lord decrees this several times in His love letter to us, and He warns us that having sex with men that are not our husband or having sex with women will result in us going to hell even if we believe in God. Well, God will tell you what is true when you read the Bible, especially Revelation 21:8. I just want to plant that seed regarding the mistruth that all believers will go to heaven when they continuously and knowingly sin without repenting.

Hell will not be the way if we repent for our sins. When we repent, we create an opportunity for God to come and save us through the redemption of Jesus because of the wounds Jesus endured. We are able to be classified as righteous (see Isaiah 53:5), and you know what the righteous will get – a crown of righteousness. That thought makes me smile, and you should smile too. We will wonder why we did not simply walk in the supernatural prior to this day, because that is how we have to live knowing that our Father's love and the presence of the Holy Spirit in us is a supernatural relationship.

Hopefully you understand that our Lord is forgiving, because even though David sins with Bathsheba and conceives a child, David is referred to as a man after God's own heart (see 1 Samuel 13:14). God knows of the sinful ways of David, but this did not keep God from seeing the heart of David as being one who wants to please God. Similarly, God knows of our sinful nature and He still loves us. Just keep seeking to do God's will, read the love letter, repent, and pray. Life will change so that you will be filled with peace that passes all understanding (see Philippians 4:7), and the reason you have access to this peace is because of Jesus. Jesus was talked about badly, but He did not respond in a fleshly manner, so we have the gift of peace (see Isaiah 53:5). Therefore, we should live in peace.

Know that our God is so gracious. He allowed Bathsheba to have a child out of wedlock, and even though this child died, we can see God's hand in her life. Yes, David fasted for the child to live, but his son did not live (2 Samuel 12:13 – 25). David did not get angry with God and blame God; instead, he acted in love and understanding of God's just decision. If you doubt this, keep looking at what happens when David goes to comfort Bathsheba after the child's death. Bathsheba gets pregnant again. She gives birth to Solomon, and Solomon becomes one of the wisest kings of Israel. Yep, that is just like God to put someone in the Bible that has a similar life to mine so that I would not feel as if the world can judge me or condemn me. Her life also exemplifies how God intervenes to help us overcome when we trust His plan.

Like Bathsheba, I had a beautiful baby named Donte'. He was concieved out of wedlock. Donte' was a sweet, loving child who always smiled whether he was going into surgery or coming out. Donte' spent most of his life in the hospital because he was diagnosed with a rare respiratory disease. Eventually, Donte' passed due to complications, but I recall praying for him continuously. I kept asking God to spare his life. I still recall the horrific morning in which I awoke to find him laying lifeless in bed. Unlike David, I did not recover from my son's death so quickly. I thought of other people who did not care for their children, yet their children were spared. I stopped going to church, and the only time in which I prayed was when I heard or saw an ambulance. Thank God for His patience, because if God had not been patient with me during the time when I was angry at Him, I would not be in the state I am in now. I am sure my parents and family prayed for me, and today I can boldly say I am the redeemed of the Lord. By the way, I now have a son named Solomon, and I did not make this connection with Bathsheba until I wrote this book. Isn't God amazing?

CHAPTER 14

Backstitch for Security

I have moments where I act unlike an heir to the throne of God. If I am honest, I do not feel like serving all the time. I do not listen to the Holy Spirit all the time. I struggle with following directions that God requires. This behavior has led me to realize that these are the moments in which I need to change my mindset. I fall short when I am experiencing long bouts of suffering and feeling overwhelmed with frustration that I have blamed on others. I have selfish moments when I say, "I want to do this my way", but God reminds me that there are others who are dealing with the same issues, so I should consider them. Although my emotions do not align with what my Lord is directing me to do, I know that He knows what is best for everyone. So, I must adjust my selfish ways to hear His voice and do what He directs me to do.

Remember, God speaks to us daily through the Holy Spirit (see Romans 8:12). We have to reconnect to the Holy Spirit within us and follow His guidance. He is our power source, and when we listen to Him, He gives us direction in every decision we make. He will even help you save money. Do you not believe me? The other day, I was at the grocery store, and when I went to purchase a product, He said, "It's cheaper at the other grocery store." God cares about everything, every penny, and every decision we make. When we listen to the Holy Spirit, we learn to become good managers over what God has given us (see Romans 8:26 - 27).

As we depend on the Holy Spirit to give us instruction, we will have insight from God, which will result in us following the will of God. Sure, we are not perfect, but we are striving to serve our purpose by making daily decisions that express the truth about how loving and caring our Lord is. If you get things wrong or if you had good intentions but things did not work out as you intended, ask your Father to forgive you and to help you see things His way. We will be victorious as we work and know the power that God has given us. This power will help us connect to our purpose. When we identify the importance of our purpose, we become stronger in the knowledge of the kingdom of God. During this search for your purpose, you will become more aware of the plans God has for your life (see Ephesians 5:12).

In the process, share your story so that others can be encouraged (see James 5:16). You matter, and your past can help others, so become free of your past. Share it with others and serve your purpose.

When we trust God, we know that He is our security and we no longer live in bondage. As we become secure in our Father, our relationship with Him begins to blossom. We also need to understand the power of relationships with others like the two Israelite spies did. They knew of Rahab's business skills as a prostitute, yet that did not keep them from going forward with seeking safety in her house. Our connection with Rahab helps us see that once we repent by changing our thinking and way of doing things so that we think on the kingdom of God, we accept that we can be instrumental in helping others. As it is important to understand that we should not think of ourselves as being better than others (see Roman 12:3), this thinking will cause us to not connect to our successful life that our Father has planned for us. Remember: your success is not based on people and what they appear to be able to do for you, but it is based on your willingness to complete what you were created to do.

You will miss the mark, but don't quit the race. There are times when I fail to hear the voice of the Holy Spirit. These are moments in which I have counted on *myself* to complete the task. I did not seek the wise Counselor that I have been given. So, I repent. Repenting requires daily consciousness of my decisions in which I have to change my way of thinking when I do not seek the advice of the Holy Spirit. It seems that I spend a lot of time repenting for saying what He told me not to say, as I am still trying to take charge when He has said to be silent. Implementing silence has become part of my daily example of how God wants me to respond when He is dealing with a situation. On these occasions, when I over-talk, I have to say, "Father, help me with this situation that I have created. I know I should have listened to Your Word and kept my mouth closed because You know better than I will ever know."

Unlike my behavior in the past, in which I made decisions on my own and never thought to ask my Lord for His help, my mindset is changing to accept that I am clueless on how God wants things to go when I strike out on my own. I am training myself to acknowledge the Holy Spirit in every decision. Within me, I have the power to be successful by obtaining what I was born to do. I just need to listen to the one in charge and stop thinking I am in charge. If you suffer from this same habit, I strongly suggest that you ask for forgiveness now and every time from this day forward. When you ask for forgiveness, smile, because you are making progress to being obedient to our Lord. Keep working to do as you were created to do, which is to be totally dependent on our Father to meet all our needs.

When I was making decisions for myself, I lived as Rahab. I exchanged my body for things that soon disappeared (see 2 Corinthians 4:18). The good thing about Rahab is that she knew when to implement a godly plan so that she could save herself and her family. That is so awesome. When we come into knowing the truth about the power we possess and change from our selfish way of thinking, things begin to unfold (see 2 Chronicles 7:14). When we realize the power that God has given us as believers and start walking as God directs us, we not only save ourselves, but we also save our families. Your family is worth you living as your Father directs you to live. Learning the truth and accepting it as part of your life saves you and your children. It allows you to provide finances for generations to come (see Proverbs 3:22).

You are a part of my family and I am a part of yours. We have our Father in heaven who cares about us while we are on earth, and He has given us the covenant, which we must follow. His rules are attached to promises that we have in the Bible. My attitude now is, "Hey, Father – guess what? I am here standing on Your Word by praying to You with these scriptures that come with a promise." The reason I do this is because every word that is written in the Bible was authorized by God through the Holy Spirit (see 2 Timothy 3:16). With the presence and guidance of the Holy Spirit, we are bound to succeed. Our Father cares about all of us. Yes, He cares about the unbelievers, too, because the Holy Spirit was sent for all (see Joel 2:28). However, there are conditions to receive the Holy Spirit. First, one must believe and confess that Jesus came to earth and was sent by God. After believing, this person must be baptized (see Mark 16:16), unless you are like John, who was born with the Holy Spirit (see Luke 1:15), or like the gentiles, who believed and spoke in tongues prior to baptism (see Acts 10:44-48). Once we are baptized, we receive our love gift, the Holy Spirit, which is from our Lord (see 1 Corinthians 12:13). What we do after receiving the Holy Spirit greatly influences how we live our lives.

As I have said, I went to church all the time when I was an adult, yet I was going to hell because I did not know the Word. I thought that all I had to do was believe, even though as a child, I had heard my father teach about those who went before Jesus and He said to depart from Him because He did not know them (see Matthew 7:21-23). Somehow, I had it twisted in my mind that He was not talking about me. Furthermore, my dad was the only one who I had heard minister to me about believers going to hell, and many other ministers' sermons boldly stated that believers do not go to hell. When you hear this message, run immediately for the door, because this is not true. The Bible clearly states that all unbelievers and those who practice lawlessness will go to hell (see Revelation 21:8). Those individuals are the believers who have been deceived by the enemy. Kick rocks, Satan; I'm done believing your lies. I'm done listening to the lies you try to play over and over in my mind. Hell is a real place, and our minds are not the place for his hellish condemnation and thoughts. We have to continue to tell this message about hell to others.

Hell has been downplayed so much that it is no longer a message that can be heard or spoken. That is how Satan tricks so many. He knows that he can downplay this truth, which allows many to continue to live in sin. I was not reading my Bible, so the truth was not coming to me. I made the choice to live blindly in sin while neglecting the evident because of my life choices. Can I get to heaven and blame the ministers for my lack of knowledge about the reality of hell? No, I can't, and neither can you! The Bible says to study to show yourself approved (see 2 Timothy 2:15), and because I knew this scripture, I was in charge of my own destiny, as I had chosen a way that seemed right to me. I did not consult my Father for insight (see Proverbs 14:12). I just did not read the Bible, which is my sword, so I was responsible for my life after death. Most importantly, I did not spend time listening to the Holy Spirit to inquire of Him what I should do. I did not try to value my time with God except on Sundays. If you are living your life as only a Sunday church-goer, please evaluate your current situation.

Time with our Lord is necessary so that He can give us words through the Holy Spirit. Because I did not value my relationship with my Father and because I did not spend time listening to the Holy Spirit, I have encountered financial loss, emotional damage, physical challenges, and spiritual setbacks. Thank goodness my Father is forgiving and longsuffering. He has forgiven me, and He speaks to me daily through the Holy Spirit. Craving to know more of God's words and the desire to understand the truth of what our Father wants to tell us will allow us to be successful, as this process takes our mind away from thinking about the things we want and need and it places our thoughts on our Father and His promises. As citizens of His kingdom under His authority, we have promises that are written for us, so when we speak to our Father, we present our case to Him so that He can intervene on our behalf. We no longer seek to gain through earthly means; instead, we seek with heavenly guidance.

It is vital to know when to stop seeking our fleshly desires and temporary things and start seeking the kingdom of God. Like Rahab, I recognized the power of God, so I am now on the winning team. I can enjoy the glory of God's presence in my life. I can share the

Word of God with others so that they will know the truth regarding the beauty of knowledge of the kingdom of God and how loving our Father is. There will be those who will not accept your message of the truth, but that is okay, because as Jesus went about spreading the good news of the kingdom of God, He was not received by His own people (see John 1:11). Hence, He spent time speaking to the gentiles and sharing the good news with them. When this happens to you and you start to feel isolated or as if everyone is against you, know that you have done as your Lord commanded you to do. Keep sharing His goodness and live in your purpose. The world needs you.

When we develop the mindset like Rahab, who recognized the power of our Lord and left her past, we can enjoy a life with someone who loves us in spite of our past. Rahab left Jericho and went to live with the Israelites. Because she allowed God to use her to do His will, Rahab's life was spared; remember that she is in the lineage of Jesus (see Matthew 1:5). Rahab made a decision during a time when others were doing their own thing, and she protected two Israelite spies and enjoyed the pleasure of our Lord in her life because not only was her life spared, but she married Salma and they had a child named Boaz. Rahab gives hope for us to live as Christ directs us to live. She gives hope to us because her life exemplifies how forgiving our Father is and how our Lord can intervene to bring success.

Accepting our Lord in our lives as the one and only true God leads to a life of kingdom-favor. Our Father is the almighty God with great strength and power. He will avenge and protect us (see Romans 12:19). He will provide for us when we trust in Him. He will honor His word, and we can live victoriously knowing that His words are flawless (see Psalm 12:6). Our Father loves us, and He wants to give us the desires of our heart, but our hearts have to be right. When our hearts are filled with love for Him, we will seek to do His will. He will grant us His favor. We just need to change from living and accepting momentary trinkets and moments of happiness through Satan's plan to living a life that gives honor to our Father. To honor our Father with love, we believe in Jesus and keep the commandments with the guidance of the Holy Spirit (see Romans 12:1).

Our willingness to be obedient allows our Father to provide for us, and He will. We just have to be willing to trust Him. Sure, there will be moments of struggle mentally, physically, financially, or even spiritually, but what we do when we are struggling will speak volumes to who we serve. Purposely dipping into sin to please your flesh or to get what you want will end up delaying your progression to receive what God has for you. I would rather wait on my Father to help me than to intentionally sin without asking for forgiveness and accepting this forgiveness. Our obedience to our Lord is key to our relationship with Him. I am so excited about how my Lord is intervening in my life, and I know that if you trust Him, your life will change too.

CHAPTER 15

"Seem" Allowance

You know how when you are getting ready to go somewhere, sometimes you cannot decide what you want to wear? You put on one outfit, take it off, and cast it to the side because it just doesn't fit right or it doesn't seem to be the right one to wear to the event. When God begins to minister to you, expect changes like this. Allow Him to structure your day around Him and His will. You don't want to *seem* as if you are in allowance with Him – you want to *be* in allowance with Him by doing as He directs. "Seem" allowance does not work. It's like having a replica of the Mona Lisa. It might seem as if it is the real thing, but it's not. It's not as valuable. It's not as detailed. Listen to hear God's voice because His words are aligned with His will. Trust me, He will speak to you and strongly make suggestions. Then, there are times when He will speak softly. It's best to do as He directs instead of needing to know why all the time.

I'm going to be honest with you and let you know that there have been times when He told me to do something and I did not do it, but I was okay after-wards. However, I could have saved myself some agony and pain. After engaging, I began to see why He made that suggestion, and had I done it when He suggested, I would have been prepared. Know that your Father will give you insight regarding people who you should or shouldn't interact with. Expect Him to let you think it is going one way only for Him to change it so that you can see His glory, meaning that He can be recognized as the one who did it for you. When He does provide for you, give Him praise. Always give Him praise, be-cause this keeps the blessings forever flowing in your life. God did it.

When people ask how you came up with the inven-tion idea, your response should be, "God did it." When you are having trouble coming up with ideas for a situa-tion and all of sudden you gain insight, remember: God did it. Give Him praise always. I cannot not stress this enough. God did it, and giving Him praise will allow the overflow to continue in your life. Live daily know-ing that even though destruction is all around you, it will not harm you (see Psalm 91). That is what happened to Rahab when she trusted in God. Her house was along the wall of Jericho, and the wall of Jericho came falling down, but Rahab's home along the wall was spared (see Joshua 6:20-23).

Do you see the miracle in this situation? Even though the wall fell, her house along the wall was not damaged. Imagine the impact you can have on a falling world if you stand for Jesus and represent God. Your decisions will not only impact your life, but will also influence the lives of others. Be willing to allow God to change you. Be willing to accept His advice when dealing with any situation. His insight can keep you safe when the world is filled with chaos.

For He has rescued us from the dominion of darkness and brought us into the kingdom of the Son He loves, in whom we have redemption, the forgiveness of sins

Colossians 1:13-14 (NIV)

Sometimes, how we entered the world and who we were raised by causes us to get stuck on questioning whether we are good enough. Let me start off by saying that you were good enough and you still are. Out of all the eggs and sperm that were occupying your mother's womb, you are one that God chose from the beginning. Jeremiah 1:5 (NIV) confirms this concept because it says, "Before I formed you in the womb, I knew you, before you were born, I set you apart; I appointed you a prophet of the nations." Maybe you are thinking, *I am not a prophet*. Perhaps you should think instead, *I am not a prophet yet*, or *I have not come into knowing this yet*.

Let me help your thinking. Have you ever wanted to do something, started to do something, or thought about going some way but went another route? Have you ever said something, and a voice told you not to do that? That was the Holy Spirit pre-warning you about the situation. When He does this, it is your glimpse into the future. He gives us pre-warning about situations and people. He gives us direction based on His future knowledge of the situation, so as you begin to receive this prophecy into your life, you will start to prophesy to others. The idea is that we must first believe and receive prophecy for ourselves before we can prophesy to others.

Your faith will lead you to see and believe that this is your gift (see Romans 12:6).Trusting in God by keeping the faith allows you to walk in your gift. Each gift that the Holy Spirit has, including prophecy, is given to us as the Holy Spirit sees fit. You also must remember that you were chosen by our Father to complete the plans He has for your life. For this reason, I would like to emphasize that it is not how you came into this earth that matters. Whether your parents wanted you or not, whether you were challenged in some way or not – that is not the reality of who you are. You are created for far greater. Think of Jesus and His purpose for coming. He is the King from heaven who used to have angels tend to His needs. He was one of authority, but He came to earth and was born not in the major hospital but in a manger – a manger with horses, sheep, and other cattle. Can you imagine the smell? Some of you probably can't even stand walking by these animals at the fair because you smell them before you see them, so imagine being born in a stable-like area with them. The first air that you breathe is full of poop – animal poop – and the stench stays with you for days.

Immediately, Jesus knew He was no longer in the palace with His Father, but His humbleness was evident from the beginning of His life. That is why we should not allow where we were raised to hold us back anymore. Let me make it even more personal. When I compare my birth to that of my siblings, I am the only one who was born in a doctor's office. I was not even born in the same city as they were, even though we lived in the same city all our childhood. The reason I was born at a doctor's office was because my father's insurance had changed. During that time, it was much cheaper for me to be born at a doctor's office than in a hospital, so my parents took the cheaper route for my birth. Does that make me less than my siblings? No, I am equal to them, because my Father says I am just as valuable as my sisters and everyone else because He does not show favoritism (see Romans 2:11).

The reason you were chosen by your Father is to serve your purpose, and that purpose is to share your gift (see Proverbs 18:16). While sharing your gift, embrace the manifold wisdom of God and make it known to the rulers and authorities in the heavenly realm what Christ Jesus our Lord has accomplished (see Ephesians 3:10-11). That is why it is vital for us to say, "God did this for us." God granted me knowledge because we identify the power and presence of God in our life. Our words are sending the message to the heavenly realms about the power of God. Shifting your thinking to serve your purpose by using your gift will lead to a life filled with promises from God. Sure, you might have to transform your mind daily, but do this knowing that your Father loves you. Transform your mind knowing that what is written in the Bible is true. Transform your mind knowing that your Father will help you. Call on Him to intervene for you. Call on Him expecting Him to save you. Call on Him knowing that He has a better plan for your life. Call on your Father, knowing that He loves you.

CHAPTER 16

Unhitched

After leaving my parents and going off to college, I got lost in myself. I tried to fit in and be like everyone else. I wanted to look like them and have nice things like them. Instead of seeing what I had in me, which was the Holy Spirit, I saw lack. This perception of myself created chaos and led me to behave more like the world instead of who God said I was. Perhaps I was angry because I was injured. During my senior year in high school, I tore three ligaments and a cartridge. My rehab wasn't that great, and I was no longer competitive. All this added to me being lost and unable to connect with God to figure out my purpose, leaving me feeling isolated. Honestly, I have always felt as if I needed to adjust to be like everyone else. When I did not know who I was or whose I was or the power within me, I did many things that did not acknowledge the truth of me and the authority given to me on earth.

Just like many of you, I knowingly committed sin. I did these things without any immediate concerns for the impact my actions had on myself or others. I only saw it as pleasing to me, and truthfully, it really wasn't pleasing to my flesh. I did it to be like everyone else. I committed these sins to please only my desire to be normal so that I could be happy – even momentary happiness was pleasing during those days. I did not embrace that I was not normal as the world describes "normal", and neither are you normal because you have the Holy Spirit in you. You have the presence of the power of your Father in you. Trying to be normal or like the world is our selfish nature. I was a true lover of myself (see 2 Timothy 3:2). See, there is danger in trying to be normal when you are far greater than normal!

Nothing about a believer is normal because we have God inside of us. Do you really understand the power in that statement? God is in you. The presence of the Holy Spirit in you is God in you because the Father, the Son, and the Holy Spirit are one (see John 10:30, John 14:26). This means that they are working on one accord to do the will of our Father. The Father, the Son, and Holy Spirit are separate, but one just like the parts of a chair. In a chair, there are different pieces, but each piece works together for one purpose, which is to provide seating. This analogy helps us see how the Father, the Son, and the Holy Spirit are one, and when we transform our minds, we become one with them by having the mind of Christ (see 1 Corinthians 2:16) and the mind of God (see Philippians 2:5-6).

Having the mind of Christ and the mind of God are powerful beliefs that will allow you to walk in faith, especially since the mind of Christ is really the mind of God. Consider how Christ walked on earth, knew how to deal with Satan, healed those in need, raised the dead, and caused even fish to be his bank accountant; that is the type of mindset we should have. That is the mindset of our God that you and I should walk in every day. What prevents us from walking in this manner is our desire to be normal; our desire to see things like the world sees them and add to the mix the principalities of darkness that constantly try to get us to think on the physical dimension instead of the spiritual dimension.

We have allowed these distractions to keep us from really serving our Father. We have prevented the world from seeing the presence of God. It is time for God's people to rise up and implement every word of the Bible into their lives. Sure, we will make mistakes, but as we progress in life, striving for the higher calling on our lives, God will open doors and show us the way. He will forgive us and tell us to keep going. It is up to us to make the change to live the life like heirs of the kingdom of God instead of living as peasants who have been disinherited. We have to move forward by accepting our purpose and acknowledge the power within us.

Having the selfish perception that we can do this by ourselves because you and I think we can grind our way to success is dangerous. The true power within us, which is the Holy Spirit, will begin to speak to us when we embrace His influence. When we listen, He will cause us to walk into the kingdom of God to see the power that we have been given as a believer. When you change your mindset from focusing on the need of things, the need for acknowledgement, and the need for pleasures for your selfish gains and begin to see that all things are yours when you implement Lord's principles into your life, you will enjoy the love and joy of the Lord. I know that growing up, I used to think that being a minister or a follower meant you had to be poor. I did not understand that our Father showed us over and over again that He is a God of more than enough not one of lack and poverty. He provided prosperity for those who kept faith in Him.

This truth is evident in the life of Job, King David, King Solomon, Bathsheba, Ruth, Isaac, and many other biblical figures. So, embrace the truth that your Father wants you to succeed. Look at the Word and see how He intervened to create prosperity in the lives of those who followed Him. When you are plagued with thoughts of lack in knowledge, wisdom, finances, health, or any aspect of your life, get your sword out and use it – it was God's breath for a reason (see 2 Timothy 3:16-17).

The Word of God will help you defeat every negative thought in your mind. Go from being carnal-minded to thinking in the supernatural realm of your Father. Study the Word of God and help His presence be known and lifted up.

When we start studying and accepting what is written in the Bible about us, we will begin to identify our gifts that God has given us. Operating in your gift will require you to break free of being normal. You will have to leave behind your natural way of doing things and focus on the spiritual way of living. As believers, we cannot deny the presence of the spiritual, and we know that it exists, yet we tiptoe around this conversation because the world does not understand it the way they should. They express their understanding of the supernatural through magic, witchcraft, sorcery, and superheroes. Yes, superheroes.

When you think about a superhero, the first thing you realize is they have powers beyond what a normal person has. They are able to engage with others supernaturally. These superheroes have taken a biblical truth and made it false so as to confuse people. The things that they are capable of doing is a replica of how Christians should engage with the world. We should walk around healing people with our touch and through the power of God. We have the greatest power, yet we crawl under rocks and hide when a person is going through an illness. Instead, we should call on the Lord, speak the Word, and they should be healed. Walking in the supernatural requires us to have faith in God beyond what we can imagine. We have to know what to do and expect things to happen. Whatever supernatural gift you have been given, use it to the intent God directed you to use it. We struggle to believe in our gifts and we struggle to see them come to pass because we don't offer a "superhero school" like the superheroes on television do for their people with superpowers. Wait – before you toss this book, let me explain.

We have Christian schools that we send our children to, but these schools never spend time teaching them about the power within them to the point where they are given time to find these powers. They are not taught how to connect to the Holy Spirit to identify their gifts. Sure, they have discussions about the Bible and the Holy Spirit, but a real Christian school needs to spend quality time teaching the children that they are not like the world because they have supernatural strength in God to do signs and wonders greater than what Jesus did. If you know of a school like this or if you know of Christians who are demonstrating their gift in the supernatural through healing and miracles, let me know. I really want to commend them for doing as Jesus said we would do (see John 14:12-14). We must cultivate our faith so that we can work in our gifts and our Father can be glorified. For our Father to be glorified, we are required to stop thinking that we did it and start praising *Him* for His presence in our lives. Believe in your heart that you possess a gift that is waiting to be released. Bring your gift forward. Save, assist, and deliver others from their afflictions and live the life you were created to live.

When you begin to identify your gift and walk in it, be very careful not to become pious or conceited. These emotions will develop as thoughts as you begin to see how powerful God works in your life. Refrain from allowing Satan to cause you to look like the world with this demeanor. When you notice that you are beginning to act like this, repent immediately and ask your Father for guidance. He will support you and help you through the process of focusing on His plan and His way of doing. Remember, if you stay humble and always give praise and recognition to your God for the gift He has given you, this will help you to constantly be aware of His presence. Perhaps you are not sure what your gift is because using your gift requires you to know yourself, and to know yourself you must know your purpose. If you do not know these things, get a journal and say a prayer every day for your Father to allow the Holy Spirit to speak to you. Then, sit quietly and listen to the Holy Spirit. You will find moments in which your mind will begin to wander, but bring it back to focus on what God directs the Holy Spirit to tell you. You might find moments in which you might start praying, but resist, because this is your time for listening (see John 16:13). To hear what the Spirit has to say, we need to practice listening to Him because we want to be aware of His voice whenever He speaks (see Revelation 2:11).

As you are seeking your gift, changing your life, or purposely listening to hear from God, negative thoughts will come to your mind. To prepare for these moments, start memorizing scriptures while washing your hands and say them. Say the same scripture until you automatically say it every time you wash your hands. Then, learn another one. These scriptures will help you fight against all negative thoughts that you may have. Implementing this practice of memorizing scriptures will help you have your sword ready to demolish every negative thought that comes from the dark world. You will understand that these thoughts of lack of self-worth and negativity are not from your loving Father. He speaks with encouragement, even when you are struggling to change or struggling to hear His voice. That is why it is important to have scriptures memorized and ready to repeat in your mind when you are on your faith journey with Christ. Knowledge of the scriptures also helps you to see who you are; they provide insight on how to gain access to our Father. Remember, by reading the Word daily and by learning scriptures, your power source, which is the Holy Spirit, will help you remember scriptures (see John 14:26) so that they will be readily available when you need them. To be able to fight the good fight of faith, you must know who you are so that you cannot become distracted, and committing these scriptures to memory will prove to be powerful, especially when you need them.

We have to be careful not to look at our Father as one who just gives without expecting anything from us. Sure, our Father will give us what we asked of Him (see Matthew 7:7), but there is a requirement to receive. He tells us to seek the kingdom of God through righteousness, joy, and peace in the Holy Spirit (see Romans 14:17) so that we can enter into the knowledge of the truth about the kingdom of God (see Matthew 7:7). Knowing about the kingdom of God helps us to become filled with the wisdom and understanding that the Holy Spirit will give us as we read the scriptures. When we read, we get a clearer understanding of our gifts and how to humbly operate in these gifts. Actively searching through the scriptures so that we can receive our daily message from our Father who loves us allows us to focus our attention on His love and ability to operate in our lives. It removes our strength from the equation and places it rightfully on our Father.

I know that I keep saying our Father loves us. Intentionally, I keep saying this so that you can understand that we have a love relationship with Him. You cannot believe unless you love Him because we believe with our heart. That is why the greatest commandment is to love the Lord with all our heart and with all our soul and with all our mind (see Matthew 22:37-38). This commandment connects us to our Father, because without loving Him, we cannot have faith. Faith is built on the principle of love, because in our heart, we proclaim our belief in God (see Matthew 10:6-10). Because of our love for God, we believe in Him and His son Jesus. Because of our belief, we are saved. Therefore, when we speak of God's love for us and our love for Him, we are expressing what our heart feels (see Matthew 12:34). Likewise, when you speak evil – this includes lies, deception, and sinful thoughts – we are not speaking out of love for our Heavenly Father, we are speaking from a worldly mind which is filled with honor for the father of lies – Satan (see John 8:42-44). Therefore, repent of your sins, go to your Father, and love on Him.

Always remember: when you go to your Father to ask Him for your needs, go with courage in your heart (see Hebrews 4:16) and know that He has a plan for your life that leads to abundance in every aspect. Your Father has everything that you need, and when we connect to Him on a spiritual level, our love for Him blossoms. Our soul – which is our heart, emotions, and mind – will be changed to see Him. To connect with Him spiritually, we must love Him with our hearts, renew our minds to the mind of Christ, and faithfully walk out our day-to-day interactions. We want to increase our spiritual connection with Him because it gives us access to His wisdom through the Holy Spirit. We cannot connect to the Holy Spirit by hearing Him speak and acting upon what He says unless our love for our Jesus and God is supernatural.

Do you know the supernatural access you have when we work on our relationship with our Lord? We have connection to some very powerful gifts that our world needs us to implement so that God can be represented on earth. When we shrink back into who we were not created to be, we do not give God a chance to be represented to the world through us and we allow the world's representative to send people spiraling down a dreadful tunnel of disappointment, unforgiveness, hopelessness, pitifulness, and destitution. Our presence as a believer has a great influence on others. When we do not display our love for our Father through our gifts, we are really acting selfishly. We are only considering ourselves when we do not share God with them. You have within you greatness which makes you supernatural. Can you boldly say that you are not normal, and that you are okay with being supernatural? That is a true statement, because as believers, we have the presence of God in us. The Holy Spirit allows us to share the love of God with others so that they can be saved. Consider that the Holy Spirit can assign power to us as He wills (see 1 Corinthians 12:8-10), and we were granted the Holy Spirit through the new covenant because of Jesus' sacrifice. Let's ask God to give us His Spirit to save others and to represent Him instead of asking God for material things for our own benefits. Yes, our Lord provides us with physical blessings, but these blessings should not be the core reason that we go to Him.

When we go to our Father, we should ask Him for the spirit of wisdom, understanding, might, counsel, the Holy Spirit, knowledge, and the spirit of the fear of God (see Isaiah 11:2-3). God's Spirit empowers us to represent Him on earth. Our Father has given us access to His Spirit, and we can have this access because of Jesus. With the Spirit of God in Jesus, we can see how to live our lives. We can see how we are to share the good news while healing and working miracles. Because of the presence of the Spirit of God in Jesus, He was able to accomplish many great things. The major difference between our ability to do as Jesus did is that He knew who was inside of Him and He knew the power of what He was operating in.

To get the gifts to operate in our lives, we must embrace in our hearts that all of our help comes from our Lord (see Psalm 121: 2-4). Many of us struggle spiritually, mentally, and physically because we do not know the truth about our power source. Jesus said that he did great things but when we recognize the power within us, we can do greater things than He did (John 14:121). Paul prayed for the people in Ephesus that they might receive the spirit of wisdom and the spirit of revelation of knowledge. When Jesus went to His Father, He brought back the gift of the Holy Spirit for us. With our connection to the Holy Spirit and God in our mind and hearts, we have access to several gifts. These gifts from the Holy Spirit are given to us as the Holy Spirit decides to give them to us. This means that there can be times when He will give us gifts as He sees them being needed. These gifts from the Holy Spirit are the gifts of wisdom, knowledge, speaking in tongues, interpreting tongues, casting out demons, prophesying, healing, and performing miracles. Many of us do not even know these gifts because we do not spend time with God. When I speak of knowing the gifts, I am not talking about knowing the gifts because you have read them in the Bible. I am saying that you know them and walk in them. You look for opportunities to walk in these gifts. When you see someone who needs healing, do you pray for them to receive healing, or do you just say that you are praying for them? When you do pray, what are your expectations?

When Jesus was presented with people who needed healing, He prayed, expecting them to be healed. We pray with this cop-out if it is Your will. Healing is God's will for us because that is what Jesus did. I cannot tell you why some people are healed and why some are not. King David's son died, my son died, and I have had friends who died. However, I can tell you that I have been delivered from cancer and there will never be another cancerous cell in my body. I believe this with all my heart because even though I went through breast cancer treatment, I know I am healed. I know that I went through that treatment for a reason and that was for God to get the glory in my complete recovery. Not knowing the important truth about the supernatural power that is in us can make life even more challenging, as we need to know the power and authority that is available to use so that we can learn who we really are. Without this knowledge, I would be fearful of saying that I am healed, especially considering that there were four of us at my job who endured cancer around the same time and I am the only one who is still alive without any recurrence. Knowing the power of the Holy Spirit can help us when we are in a situation in which we need Him to intervene in our lives. Honestly, we need Him in every aspect of our lives so that we can think and operate with a spiritual mindset instead of a worldly one.

When we are transforming our minds from anxiety, depression, guilt, deep sorrow, anger, or bitterness, releasing our past thoughts and teachings of bondage gives us complete wholeness into our Father's love. Our thoughts must embrace that our Father is forgiving and that we are forgiven. That is why I can say that I am forgiven for aborting my children. There is no need for anyone to try to say anything differently to me, as they would have to argue with our almighty God. Since He approved every word in the Bible, we cannot pick and choose the ones we want to follow even though we might not agree with them. Therefore, according to our Father's love letter to us, the only sin that is not forgiven is blasphemy against the Holy Spirit (see Mark 3:28-29). For years I was not sure what blasphemy was, so I want to provide the Bible's description of this unforgivable sin.

Blasphemy against the Holy Spirit, according to what Jesus said, is claiming or making statements against the power of the Holy Spirit when He does His assigned job (see Matthew 3:23-27). In other words, when the Holy Spirit works through us in any of the gifts, it is a sin to identify these gifts as power from Satan. You see, giving Satan credit for what God does is blasphemy (see 2 Corinthians 12:1-11). Although I committed adultery and murder along with many other sins, I do not have to hold my head low or think less of myself, as I know the truth: I am forgiven. You are forgiven too.

Our Father's love for us extends beyond the earthly love that we demonstrate in our earthly relationships. His love for us is supernatural. It is a love that overlooks our sins when we ask Him for forgiveness. That is why it is important to grab hold to the love that our Father has for us. We must look at things from His all-knowing abilities. When we do, we realize that even though He knew we would still sin and not do his will, He gave us a gift as a representation of His love for us. He gave us Himself, which is the Holy Spirit. We have God in us, and He is powerful. He has an assignment to help us and He speaks to us so that we can know what God wants us to do and how God wants us to act. The Holy Spirit is a gift of love from our Father. Everything our Father has done for us was out of love. Our almighty King has blessed us with His presence and His power through His Holy Spirit. Because He and my Father are one, I am one with them. Together, with a spiritual mindset, I am able to overcome all obstacles and live with my Father's grace that covers me daily.

I truly desire to write how life changing and powerful our lives should be with our Father living in us so you can receive His power, His presence, and His love. Knowing God requires us to transform our mind from thinking of life in this worldly mindset to thinking on a higher level that is spiritual. Our spiritual power within us wants to bring this clearly to our soul so that we will no longer be confused or bound. It will become automatic for us to make decisions that are what God wants us to do. We will immediately hear the voice of the Holy Spirit and follow Him. The Holy Spirit's presence in us is far greater than you and I can imagine. That is why it is written that our Father can do more than we can think or imagine (see Ephesians 3:20).

Imagine far more for your life. Imagine more of a life with God than a life of the world. Think of what you have seemingly accomplished without God and realize that those accomplishments that you think were done without Him really were not without Him. He allowed you to accomplish those things and that was without you really knowing the presence of Him in your life. When we focus on loving God and doing what God directs us to do, we can achieve greatness through Him. I am so excited about my life and where God is going to take me, as I know each step will exhibit His glory.

Acknowledge the power within you. He has given it to you because this powerful connection will give you insight into living as an heir to the kingdom of God. When you embrace and acknowledge the Holy Spirit, all feelings of guilt and shame will be demolished. Honestly, every ungodly thought that comes to you is defeated by the God in you. I am not saying that you won't have thoughts that challenge your self-worth. What I am saying is that these feelings and thoughts are not from God. They are Satan's way of manipulating the truth so that you will never know who you really are. He does not want you to know the authority that you have on earth as a citizen of the kingdom of God. Satan is a bully who wants to demolish your self-esteem and keep you from walking in the power of God. He wants to keep you from flowing in the Spirit because your bondage prevents you from saving others who are struggling, and it keeps you from knowing who you are in Christ. Walk away from his trickery and love on your Father. He loves you and He cares for you. You are His child, and your Father will never disown you when you confess your love for Him while denouncing your sin.

Satan is a jealous spirit that wants to keep you from walking away from the prison of sin. He wants to extend your sentence even though he has no power to do so. He sets out to attack all of us. He even went after Jesus at a time when He was seeking his Father's advice, and if he went after Jesus, we are all subject to the enemy's persecution. It is how we respond to his malicious thoughts that make the difference. Consider Jesus' predicament. When Jesus finished fasting for forty days, Satan immediately began to try to manipulate him. This invasion of Satan into Jesus' life clearly demonstrates how Satan seeks an opportune time to inflict doubt and confusion. If you notice, Satan tells Jesus a scripture from Psalm 91:11-12. He reminds Jesus that God will command His angels concerning Him to guard Him in all His ways.

Satan told Jesus that the angels would lift Him up in their hands so that He would not strike His foot against a stone. Notice the deceptiveness of Satan. Satan did not tell Jesus Psalm 91:13, which clearly states that we will tread on the great lion and the serpent. He only told part of the scripture, and he told it out of context. Satan is the father of lies (see Matthew 8:44). He has been lying to you and me all this time. We have openly received his lies and lived without knowing the truth about how to live victoriously. It is time to pay attention to how the devil comes at us because he will use the same strategy repeatedly because he knows human patterns. Break the pattern and stop allowing him to have the position of a counselor in our lives.

Start believing today that you will not be overcome with the lies of the principalities of darkness, but rather, you will walk into the kingdom of God knowing the truth of who you are and that your Lord loves you. Embrace that you have supernatural power in you that advocates for you in Heaven. Live knowing why Jesus came to earth, which was to put things back in order, as this shows our Father's deep love for us. Jesus brought back the kingdom of heaven to earth. He brought back the way we should operate in the Spirit of God. Jesus brought back harmony between us and our Father.

Remember, the kingdom of heaven is on earth. The presence of the Holy Spirit, your direct connection to God, is the kingdom of God (see Romans 8:26). In other words, wherever God is in us is the Kingdom of God, and wherever the almighty God is, that is heaven. Live life full of your Father's love for you and walk knowing that God in you is the power to rule over every demonic attack that comes after you.

Know that the principalities of the dark spiritual world know when we are struggling, but believe that once you get the truth about the kingdom of God, you will hunger for more understanding (see Matthew 13:33). Accept the power within you that was delivered to us by Jesus. He brought you the Holy Spirit, and with the presence of the Holy Spirit, you have power. Embrace the Holy Spirit in you and love on God so that you can live in peace, victory, and forgiveness.

CHAPTER 17

Love Conquers All

When I had an abortion, I did not understand the struggle my mom had prior giving birth to me. You see, my mother had several miscarriages, and with each pregnancy, I am sure the fear of death tried to overtake her thoughts. Likewise, I had a miscarriage and a premature birth in which my son, Donte', who was born on my birthday, died after four years. With these challenging experiences in my mind, my past abortions plagued me, trying to tell me that I was being punished for having an abortion and that God had not forgiven me. Daily, I battled the thought that God would never forgive me for having an abortion, and I lived with this burden of guilt for years. I was burdened with guilt because I was listening to the wrong messenger. I had not accepted that my Father loved me past my sins. Just to make sure I didn't see God loving me, Satan kept placing thoughts of disaster and unworthiness in my mind. Satan the accuser is always looking for opportunities to condemn us, especially when we are trying to rationalize why we are currently dealing with loss. This loss may include financial, emotional, family, relationship, or friendship. When dealing with any form of loss, Satan is there ready to insult us with a message of negativity. Someone might even say that I deserve not to have children because of my abortions. The reality is I used to think this too. However, it is important to remember that we do not know why we encounter suffering in life as God reminded Job that He is the creator with great wisdom, and He uses His wisdom to direct our lives (see Job 38-42) . We know that Job endured great suffering even though he was righteous. With his perils in mind and God's response, we should ask God to comfort us when we feel pain and allow the Holy Spirit to guide us through with patience and confidence (see Romans 8:24-25).

In the process of trying to live for Christ, I made some changes, and I felt these changes would help my relationship with God. First, I got married prior to giving birth to Donte'. While I was not married to his father, I had decided to change my ways by trying to do what appeared right. This required me to iron out things that often caused buckling in my thoughts. In other words, I had to renew my mind because my past identified areas that needed addressing like my love for sex, so I got married. I also became active in helping others. I was working in the church and teaching elementary school in an area that had issues with keeping teachers. While serving others in this capacity, my son died. After my son's death, I became angry with God, and I did not want to hear anything He had to say. I was not like King David, and I struggled with the fact that God had forgiven me because Satan kept me from accepting God's forgiveness with thoughts of inadequacies. I was angry with God because I did not see how He was demonstrating His love for me by allowing my son to die, and I justified my anger because I was working with parents who did not value their children like I thought they should. They had excuses after excuses for not engaging in their child's education, and some of their excuses infuriated me. How could God care more for their children than mine? See how selfish I was, even during my affliction? I should have asked myself how I could help parents educate their children. It was my responsibility to help them, not judge them.

Years later, my anger turned into accepting God's decision like King David did. This acceptance meant that I had to acknowledge that I do not know God's plan just like others don't. However, I do have to deal with the impact the experience had on my life. To help me address my hurt and anger, I knew I had to work on my relationship with God. This meant I had to come to the point of believing that no matter what happens, I can trust God's wisdom. Trusting God's wisdom doesn't mean I don't feel the pain of the loss, but it does mean that I do not see the situation as the ending of who I am. Instead, I see it as an opportunity to extend my faith in the Lord. With this in mind, I would like to apologize to everyone who has tried to have a child but couldn't, and I send my deepest love to those have lost a child. I understand your pain and the burden this lost might have created for you. From this day forward, let us allow God to love us when dealing with loss so that we can embrace His presences in every aspect of our lives. This requires faith in His wisdom.

God's wisdom is far greater than mine and yours, and I am learning from my life experiences that God's timing is purposeful. His wisdom is for His glory on earth so others can see His strength. There might be times in which I feel uncomfortable because things are not exactly how I want them, but it is important to keep the faith because my faith demonstrates my love for Him. Trusting God in this manner is challenging as our human nature seeks to be in control. For this reason, we must suppress our human nature and allow our spirit to be guided by the Holy Spirit.

I know that I was wrong for having the abortion, but I do not have any form of guilt for my decision, because God has forgiven me. That is how much He loves me, and I had to embrace that Donte' was no longer suffering on earth. God knows what is best. As a result, I have a better relationship with Him, and I do not see Him as someone who is waiting for me to do wrong so that He can punish me. I know that He is not out to destroy me, but instead He wants to love me daily. Weeping may endure for a moment, but joy will surely come if we keep believing (see Psalm 30:5). Come on, joy! Let's dance and celebrate because we believe in our Father's wisdom, and His wisdom directs us to fulfill His desires.

Our Father forgives. Our Father cares. We must serve Him and know that how we deal with life's challenges impacts how we will live on earth as either powerless or powerful. Let us choose to live in the power of the kingdom of God. Let us accept the presence of the Holy Spirit in our lives and allow the Holy Spirit to guide us. Our Father loves us and He forgives us, so walk in the glory of the kingdom of God and learn of His ways so you can know how life as a believer is supposed to function. Know that you are forgiven. Embrace that we are our Father's children who make mistakes, but as heirs of His kingdom, we have His favor, forgiveness, and love.

Extra! Extra!: Get Your Spiritual Covering Today!

When we see Jesus as King, it helps us to understand the power He displayed on Earth. It is also important to embrace that He is the King and likewise, we are kings (see Revelation 1:6). Jesus is a child of God like us (see John 1:12-13). Jesus had God in Him and so do we (see Ephesians 1:13 - 14). Because Jesus operated knowing who He was, He was a great example for us. He exemplified how we should live with the power and presence of the Holy Spirit in us. Perhaps you are thinking, *But Jesus did not sin.* This is true. However, as believers, we need to move away from the mental bondage of sin to freedom in God. We serve in this same authority as Jesus did. We even have the mind of Christ, which comes from the Holy Spirit (see 1 Corinthians 2:16). We must think like Jesus and accept the responsibility to serve others by sharing love, joy, and peace in the Holy Spirit.

Perhaps in the past we have tried to live life without the Holy Spirit guiding us. We did not acknowledge His active presence in our lives or we gave Him limited access. Because of our actions, we do not exercise our strength in the Spirit to get things done, and this can be attributed to our lack of faith. Our lack of faith prevents us from connecting to our source. We are encouraged to be strong in the Lord and His mighty power (see Ephesians 6:10). We cannot be strong if we lack faith and try to live without the guidance of the Holy Spirit, because with the Holy Spirit, we have the authority on earth to bind and lose things (see Matthew 18:18). What have you been binding and loosing? Have you been keeping the Holy Spirit bond with limited access in your life?

Close Your Mouth and Stitch Your Lips

As rulers of this world, we have dominion, and with dominion comes power. Understanding how our power works requires us to reflect on how the earth was created. God spoke and things were created. Likewise, our words are powerful. As a matter of a fact, our words are so powerful that they can either bring life and death into existence (see Proverbs 18:21). When we speak of life and death, we are saying that our words can make a dream a reality or it can destroy the dream.

Our words can encourage someone to want to keep going or they can destroy them. Our words can make a sick person better or they can destroy them. Our words are powerful. That is why it is vital for us to stay connected to the Holy Spirit. When we are connected to the Holy Spirit, He will limit the words that we let fly out of our mouths, and when we begin to have a conversation that we should not be engaging in, the Holy Spirit will suggest that we shut up. That's powerful, because our tongues are difficult to tame (see James 3:1-12). However, with the Holy Spirit in us, all things are possible. As you change your WARdrobe, remember to allow the Holy Spirit to help you keep your big mouth closed.

Expect the Holy Spirit to be honest. He has told me to be quiet many times when I wanted to prove my point, share an idea, or over-talk. Apparently, what I wanted to say would not have contributed as much as my silence. Accept opportunities to remain silent and do not let anyone cause you to deny or act contrarily to the power of the Holy Spirit that rests, rules, and abides in you (see 2 Corinthians 13:14). Remember that you are in a spiritual battle, and at any point, these spirits may come at you to try to demolish what your Father has given you. Satan might use your family, friends, colleagues, or anyone who has a mouth to impose upon your walk with your Father.

Have you ever said, "I'm not going to sin again. I'm done. I quit"? There have been many times in which I have recognized my sinful ways and said that I am not going back to that lifestyle again. I have even told my friends that I am through having sex without being married to the guy. I honestly meant those words. My friends and I even made an agreement to stop sleeping with the guys we were dating. Perhaps you have said this same thing about the sin that you continue to commit. Whether it's drug addiction, lying, sexual immorality, or stealing, you wanted to stop. You might have even stopped for a period of time, but you found yourself coming back, indulging in the very same act of sin. You might have even wondered how you ended up back with the guy you swore you would never see again or how you ended up taking another hit. Remember, we are in a spiritual battle, and because the dark spirit returns and finds us empty of the truth regarding how to live like the Word of God says, he comes back to invade us. Yes, we spoke the word, and we meant what we said, but we did not put into action the eviction process that would keep these trespassers from returning.

To keep these spirits from returning, we need to put in a plan that will allow us to be successful. When I made the commitment to stop intentionally sinning, I did not do anything differently. I mean that I did not read my Bible. I did not pray. I did not meditate on the Word. I suppose I was really trying to do this by myself, because I did not even consult with the Holy Spirit on how to move forward. The Holy Spirit is needed every day of our lives to help us fight this spiritual battle. He speaks to us and helps us when we need Him. The Holy Spirit is the power within you that allows you to tread, trample, overcome, and succeed. He gives us access to the kingdom of heaven, as He represents us in heaven and allows the presence of the kingdom of God to dwell on earth.

You have been given the ability to live your purpose by your Father. He wants you to achieve what He created for you to do. The only way to guarantee that you will be successful in achieving this goal is for you to seek the kingdom of God (see Matthew 6:33). Remember, we seek the kingdom of God through love, joy, and peace in the Holy Spirit. In other words, we need to discontinue counting and depending on ourselves, others, and things and start seeking our heavenly Advisor, who is the Holy Spirit, so that He can give us direct information from God. Our Father knows your future. His plan provides you with success to complete the plans He has for your life. In His plans for you, you will prosper and not be harmed. You will have hope in the future and good health to enjoy your life (see Jeremiah 29:11). Trust your Father's plan for your life and follow His principles of seeking the kingdom of God by reading the Bible and praying continuously. As you implement these key factors into your life, your Father will give you the secrets that are waiting for you (see Luke 8:10).

There is great power within you – walk in it, know who you are, and believe the truth of who your Creator has said you are. To make God real in our lives, we need to seek the kingdom of God – or shall I say you need to seek who God is. How? When we read the Bible, the Holy Spirit will give us insight about the verses that we read. In your reading, you will learn how the kingdom of God operates and you will see your responsibility in implementing your faith as it causes things to manifest. You will learn about your gifts that your Father has given you and your faith will increase when you begin to see the kingdom life demonstrated through you. When we work in the kingdom of God, we are causing things to function as God designed them to operate.

As we allow the Holy Spirit to speak to us and as we go forth in life doing what our Father authorized us to do, we will take back the dominion from Satan. We can no longer allow what Jesus Christ did for us to exist only in the scriptures. We must live daily, exhibiting the power of God. When we do not live as our Father directs us to live, we are limiting His ability to be seen. We are limiting God's presence and power in our lives. Jesus came to bring us the kingdom of God, so when we do not walk knowing the truth, we are demonstrating distrust in what our Father says about us. Within us, we have the power to trample the serpent's head. Live under the authority of our righteous Father. Love Him and allow Him to work His power in you so that you show the world the power your Father has granted you and He can get the glory. It is your responsibility to walk boldly on earth while expressing your love for your Father by doing His will for your life.

Go forward knowing that nothing can hold you back when you walk with your Father. Mistakes, sins, errors, and misfortunes have no power over you. Sure, Satan will try to tell you that you deserve punishment, but remember that this is his death sentence that he wants to impose upon you. You are not your past. Our past is for us to learn from while moving forward to show others how merciful our almighty God is.

Consider how a company operates. When they identify an area that is not productive, if the company wants to survive, it must learn from this area and move forward. Likewise, your past might be full of many areas in which you would have preferred not to have engaged, and if you had an opportunity, you would have responded differently, but the beauty of coming into the knowing of the truth of who you are is that you are not bound to those errors. Learn and progress. Move forward. Keep focused on your purpose and your goals in the kingdom of God. Keep seeking God and understand the truth of the power within you. You have the power to overcome all obstacles because you are connected to God. With the Holy Spirit in our hearts and minds, we have the faith to shift how the world sees our heavenly Father (John 14:26, Hebrews 6:7-13). We can enjoy life with God, walk in peace, and bask in the joy of the Holy Spirit. In other words, allow the Holy Spirit to be your guide in every decision. Start spending quality time sitting quietly and allowing the Holy Spirit to speak to you. This time creates an opportunity for growth in every area of your life, including wisdom, understanding, knowledge, and proper connections in the areas where you need insight. You will also begin to recognize His voice, making it easier for you to receive His instruction, guidance, and protection.

Below is a prayer that reminds me that I am not guided by situations, but by the Holy Spirit. It helps set my day for purpose driven by God. Consider saying it daily and sitting quietly to hear what the Holy Spirit has to say. Take notes and reread them to remind you of the messages He gave you from your Father:

"Holy Spirit, with Your active presence in my life, provide guidance, direction, and protection so I can make good decisions based on biblical principles. I receive Your insight in every decision I make. Amen."

CHAPTER 18

Your Cheeks Are Showing

As you are listening to the Holy Spirit, you will start to see how changes are needed in your life. I had made several changes even though prior to the changes I thought I was doing well. Imagine my shock when my time with the Holy Spirit revealed that I needed to make more changes. Of course, my first response was, "I am changing." Yes, I said that with an attitude. I even defended my life choices with the One who knows my heart. I reminded the Holy Spirit how I was paying attention to what I say and how I acted. I am sure the Holy Spirit was laughing and saying, "Is that all this girl thinks she needs help with? She really has a problem." I am sure the Holy Spirit knows about all my issues, as He lives in me, but I was thinking I was doing well. Then, He said, "I need you to implement this change immediately. Before you open your mouth, I need you to pause, pray, and proceed." Now I was thinking, *Well,*

I guess I do need a little more help, because rarely do I pause, pray, and proceed (see Luke 18:1). I usually just proceed with whatever emotion or thought that first comes to my mind. Selfish me. Can you imagine? I am sure that most of my responses were based on me thinking only of myself. Holy Spirit, help me, because I thought I was doing well. Apparently not!

As I reflect on my notes that I took that day after writing "Pause. Pray. Proceed", I wrote, "Do not give up. I am with you." Now, if you go and read Luke 18:1, it says just that. It reminds us to always pray and to never give up. God had given me these words in my quiet time with the Holy Spirit. There is no way I will ever stop having my time with the Holy Spirit. He is my secret weapon and true gift from God. He reminded me of the Scriptures so that I would be able to proceed in life successfully as God had designed me. I am telling you, this confirms that the Holy Spirit speaks to me and that I can hear Him. Likewise, the Holy Spirit will speak to you, too. Expect to hear Him and follow His instruction. Be mindful that when you start listening for the voice of the Holy Spirit, Satan will try to tell you that God is not speaking to you, but do not be deceived by his deceitful ways. You are your Father's and you will hear His voice (see John 10:27).

I am so excited about my life, and even though I have to work on myself, I know that it is for a reason. I must know how to interact with God's people and not think that the president of a company's life is more valuable than the person who lives on the streets. God is helping me see who He wants me to be and He has allowed me to meet people so that He could show me that there is a purpose for my life and that I need to work on me to get to the next level. My Father reminds me that He has me in this position during this season so that I can learn the power that is within me, and that power is not myself, but it is the Holy Spirit (see 1 Corinthians 9:10).

While you think you have it together, know that a test is coming. Please don't think that I have got this together, because I have areas God is showing me that need repairing. I can merely reflect on yesterday to see how I could have responded differently.

Yesterday, there was an elderly lady who was looking for cream corn in the same store I was shopping in. I know I could have probably talked to her to assist more, but I wanted to hurry up and get out of the store. However, let me tell you the story before I start justifying my behavior. While shopping, I noticed the elderly lady standing in the aisle looking at items. I wanted her to hurry up and get out the way, but I waited while remaining silent and watched her scan the items. Notice my attitude: even in silence, I was out of order and acting selfish. Although I considered her age, I did not internalize that she might need help – selfish me!

Then, when she walked away, she gave me a job to do – find her some creamed corn. Inside, I wanted to tell her she should probably just take what they had, which was whole kernel corn because things were scarce due to the coronavirus pandemic, but I kept my big mouth closed. Thank goodness! I also did not pause, pray, and proceed. This would have been a great opportunity to implement this concept.

As I was glancing at the corn, I noticed two cans of cream style corn. I walked over to her and placed them in her hands. She asked me where I found them, and I showed her the area. There were not any more left, and she quickly let me know that they were not the brand she wanted. With this comment, I walked away, leaving her to decide on what she wanted to do. Surely she was aware that the shelves were bare. However, she knew what she wanted and was not interested in any substitutes. I am not aware if she kept what I found or not, because shortly afterwards, I was faced with another opportunity to be Christ-like. Thankfully, that time I remembered to be kind.

When God speaks to you through the Holy Spirit, expect to change. Expect to have opportunities for God to show you how you need to work on *you*. You will be presented with many occasions that will exhibit your inner self, and if you are like me, the pride of life is an area that you will have to work on constantly, because God loves us all equally. There is no hierarchy. To help you when faced with situations, remember to pause, pray, and proceed.

Many of our thoughts are clouded with misconceptions about the truth of who we really are. Our mindsets are overpowered by self-centered concepts that bog us down with ideas that do not help us connect with our true purpose. Greed, selfishness, personal satisfaction, and stinginess limit our commitment to allow us to walk in the beauty of who we are. This attitude keeps us in bondage, as the truth of our destiny is chained to thoughts and behaviors that never allow us to embrace the truth of the power we have. For this reason, temporary things encapsulate our footsteps into a destiny and keep us from moving forward to a place of satisfaction and peace. As a result, we do not care about the needs of others, as we are too broken and too selfish to think beyond our painful thoughts and memories to see how we can positively influence others as we embrace our purpose. Sure, we might give the guy on the corner a quarter or we might listen to someone who needs our help, but what people really need is for us to serve our purpose in love.

In order to serve your purpose, you need to know your purpose. Knowing your purpose really requires you to look at your life as a journey in which you endured many challenges and overcame them all with

God's help. Yes, you overcame them, because if you hadn't, you would not be seeking to find your purpose in an effort to serve others. Without this mindset, we fail to accept our purpose. Listen: you are extremely gifted with a purpose to overcome all challenges that present themselves in your life. However, many times, when we are presented with our purpose, we see it as an opportunity to exercise our right to choose. We see serving our purpose as a challenge and we justify not doing as we have been gifted by satisfying the world with excuses for not proceeding with a purposeful life. When you exercise your right to accept or deny your walk in your purpose, it has a great impact on yourself and others within the world who need someone like you to share your purpose so that they can reach their destiny. You see, your purpose is not for you, that is the root of your selfish thoughts. Acknowledge your purpose as a means to serve others so that you can help them see that there are other options. There are many people that need to know that someone cares about them enough to share beyond their hurt and limits to save them. Will you be that person?

Your purpose is not forced upon you. You have to take it and the knowledge of it to do something with it. What you do with that knowledge influences your outcome. Your purpose can be used to help others who are connected to other people. It is like the yeast in bread dough. Although it is small in comparison to the amount of flour added to the mixture, it has a great impact on that tasty banana nut bread. In other words, compared to the end results, what you have been assigned as your purpose might seem small, but it has the ability to help others rise beyond their current situation. What happens to the dough after the ingredients have been mixed? The dough is put in the fire of the oven to become something greater than what it was when it was just one simple ingredient (see Luke 13:20-21). You see, that is the kingdom mindset. You take the gift that you have been given and you use it to help make something greater. You are not thinking only of yourself. You are sharing the truth of your journey to save others. Your willingness to share helps you overcome your struggles and allows you to walk in your purpose.

Because individuals like Rahab the prostitute served their purpose despite the fact that they had lived a sinful life, I can do the same. Rahab only had to repent, have faith, and trust that God was the almighty God. The same thing is true about you. Repent by changing your thinking. Serve your purpose and help others become stronger in knowing who they are and why their lives matter to the kingdom of God.

CHAPTER 19

WARdrobe Change

*The night is nearly over; the days are almost here. So let us
put aside the deeds of darkness and put on the armor of light.*

Romans 13:14 (NIV)

Because of our Father's great love for us, He gave us
an amazing gift that reassures us that we are not going
to be trudging through life alone and uncared for. His
gift of armor helps us to overcome all obstacles that we
encounter. To receive this gift and get the benefits, we
have to take action. Our Father says, "Here – take it, and
put it on." If our Father commands that we take action
by putting on the full armor of God, this indicates that
we can take it off, because what we put on can be removed. When we take off the armor that God has given
us, we are engaging in battle without consideration of
our exposure to sin (see Romans 6: 15-18). Sin exposure
is far worse than sun exposure, and if we willingly apply suntan lotion to protect us from the sun, surely we
should apply the armor of God to protect us from sin.

However, I must admit that I have enjoyed many days at the beach with suntan lotion and was clueless to where my armor was located. I had sun protection, but not *sin* protection.

Removal of the armor is a purposeful action that we do, and it allows Satan to have a straight shot at our soul. Sometimes, we might even have the armor with us, but we do not use it appropriately. As a result, we start to live in sin, doubt our Father, and get off track from God's plan for our lives. Slowly, our armor becomes unimportant, resulting in us living sinfully. When we begin to live without our armor, we run the risk of being judged instead of receiving the mercy of God (see James 2:12). When we remove our full armor, what do we have on? We have on our Sunday's best, which only covers our flesh, and it leaves us bearing our sins. Without the armor, we have our own sinful ways because we were born in sin (see Psalm 51:5), which means we are not living our lives as God commanded. We all know that we cannot serve two gods. We either love one or hate the other (see Matthew 6:24). Therefore, removal of our armor means we are now serving the prince of darkness (see Matthew 6:24, John 8:44-45). In order to live as directed by God, we need to put on the whole armor so that we can overcome all obstacles that we encounter. Without the entire armor on, we are subject to live our lives as sheep without a shepherd, doing things that cause destruction to ourselves.

For many years, I have lived without the full covering of God's armor. I am so sick and tired of living life like this. During those years without proper weaponry, I self-inflicted many injuries. Everything I tried to accomplish through sin resulted in me still experiencing that same lack. However, my Father has willingly healed each injury because He loves me. He loves you too and wants to heal you. Let me reassure you that He will heal you, but Satan will try those same mind games to keep you distracted from God's plan. Don't fall for them. Constantly renew your mind to think like Jesus because you have the mind of Christ because of the Holy Spirit that lives in you (see 1 Corinthians 2:16).

Without the full armor of God, as you can imagine, I lived life as I chose and did what I wanted to do even though I was dressed to look my best every Sunday when I went to church. My Sunday's best left me vulnerable to living in darkness even though I had the Holy Spirit in me, believed that Jesus died for my sin, and believed that God raised Him from the dead. Believing in our supernatural Father, His Son, and His power limited my understanding of the strength within me. I needed to learn to love my Father and want to do what is pleasing to Him. These love walks took some time because my desires to have what I wanted without Him needed to be replaced with His love for me and my love for Him.

There were many days in which I kicked the Holy Spirit to the curb so that I could do what I wanted to do. My behavior grieved and quenched the Holy Spirit, which prevented me from hearing God's voice. I knowingly did this because I can recall when I first started smoking marijuana, He would talk to me and tell me to quit because my behavior would make it more challenging to stop. Like I said earlier, with each puff, I kept thinking, *I can beat this habit anytime*, so I would stop for a period of time only to end up going back to it. However, God spoke to me that day as I was smoking marijuana in the bathroom – I heard the Holy Spirit clearly say, "Stop smoking", *and* it was confirmed by my partner when I walked into the bedroom. I did not stop because my partner asked me; I stopped because the Holy Spirit spoke to me and I heard Him. The Holy Spirit simply confirmed His message by giving my partner the exact same words. My Father spoke to me that day, I heard Him, and I repented by changing my selfish thinking to thinking more towards what God would expect and want me to do. In the process of changing, I began to put on the whole armor of God and seek the kingdom of God. I wanted to know more about Him and how I should live. Through this transformation, my life's purpose was identified, as I am now sharing the message of God with you (see Romans 12:1-2).

As believers, we know that Satan and his demonic spirits are always seeking to attack us, especially when we begin to learn of the kingdom of God and walk in the ways of God (see Matthew 12:31-43). He wants to remove this truth because knowledge of the kingdom gives us understanding about our connection to our Father. Satan seeks to completely demolish our belief in the power that is available to all believers when we trust our Father. He strives to make every thought doubt what our Father says, and this has always been his plan from the beginning of time. His desire to get us to mistrust our Lord is evident when we listen to how he deceived Eve and how he constantly tries to persuade us. Of all the things that we can listen to, Satan is clearly one spirit that we should recognize as a voice of lies. He always has suggestions that contradict everything our Father says. However, as we begin to study the kingdom of God, we receive a clearer understanding of the God in us, which is the Holy Spirit. The Holy Spirit is given to believers as God sees. The transmission of the Holy Spirit is given through birth (see Luke 1:13-15), through touch (see Acts 19:6), when asked (see Luke 11:13), and when one hears the Word and believes, even though they have not been baptized (see Acts 10:44-47).

Through the presence of the Holy Spirit, God is showing us that He can intervene in our lives in many ways when we submit to Him. Submitting to our Lord challenges our past thoughts or beliefs, but is this not really who God is – One who challenges our flesh so that we can see His wondrous power? So often, we try to see Him as one dimensional with one way of intervening and proving His presence in our lives, when in reality, there are so many avenues that He has access to and can interject from. Allowing God to be in your life through total submission places you in alignment with His will, not yours. We have to totally trust Him and accept when He changes our life's direction so that He can be glorified. He is our Lord. He is our King. He has dominion overall.

Trusting God and believing beyond our limits that we place on Him allows God to be the almighty presence in our lives without limitations. Ask God to open your eyes and allow His truth to be revealed in your life. This struggle is not yours; it belongs to Him (see 2 Chronicles 20:15). Give every challenge to Him and say, "Now God, show up as You will." Record what transpires so that you can encourage others and stay encouraged along the journey. Fight every thought of doubt with faith in God. Bring scripture to mind, say it, and tell God you trust Him, for when our Father helps us, it will be His meticulous intervention that will reveal the truth of who He is and how we are to serve our purpose by walking in faith and trusting Him. Set yourself aside and be willing to receive every challenge you encounter as God's way of saying, "I know that you know the truth of who I am, so let's go forward. Keep your dream I gave you in your heart and believe in my victorious outcome for your life."

God's promises are not empty and void like that of man's. His promises have value and power. His promises are trustworthy, so believe in them. Cling to them and study them so that when you are in a mind battle with the spirits of darkness, those scriptures will reassure you of the promises and power of God. Live a victorious life with God's promises in your forethoughts so that God's Word will always be ready to defend you when the enemy comes to attack you. Celebrate with praise when under attack by renewing your mind with the promises of God.

There are days when I have to constantly tell myself that my Lord loves me. I also listen to sermons and gospel music that reset my mind. I implement these plans because I know that the dark spirits are trying their hardest to distract me to throw me off track. For years, I acted like a dog led astray by the scent of what appeared to be the right way. Now, I strive to be tenacious in the word of God by believing what God has given me in my heart. I believe His truth over Satan's lies. It is imperative for us to believe in God no matter what, because we want to experience a life like Job – full of spiritual and physical prosperity which is given when we keep the faith despite our current circumstances. Grab hold to the knowledge of the kingdom of God and allow Him to show you His love.

When we seek to understand the kingdom of God, we gain a better understanding of how to operate in life as our Father's child. We are God's chosen children, as the Holy Spirit is present in us (see Romans 8:16). Therefore, Satan goes to great lengths to make sure that we do not understand this powerful connection that we have with our Father. The Holy Spirit prepares and assists when we are dealing with spiritual attacks. The Holy Spirit also speaks to us when we read the scriptures to help us get a better understanding of the love letter our Father gave us. When we are dealing with situations, the Holy Spirit will remind us of the message from our Father (see John 14:26). Because Jesus had the Holy Spirit in Him (see Isaiah 11:2), He was prepared for the attacks from Satan. Actually, Jesus teaches us just how to deal with Satan. With every word that Satan said to Jesus, Jesus replied with a scripture. Also, notice Satan's demeanor after being defeated. He was like, "I'll be back another day."

Although it might appear as if this was the only time that Jesus dealt with Satan, we have to consider that Satan and those demonic spirits were always in other people. This resulted in Jesus casting out demons, rebuking Peter, and dealing with the pharisees. Each spirit was defeated because Jesus was well prepared with the weaponry God had given Him. Likewise, we need to be prepared with our armor. Just like Paul warns us in Ephesians to put on our whole armor, it is important to know that Jesus also was well equipped. He wore a sash of faithfulness and a belt of righteousness (see Isaiah 11:5) so that He could minster to the people the goodness of the kingdom of God. If Jesus armored up, then surely we need to do so as well. These are good gifts that our Father has for us. It is important for us to receive the gifts that He has given us and implement them so that we can live as He promised.

When I lived my life as I chose even though I was a believer, I had removed my armor to satisfy the desires of my flesh. As a matter of fact, I kicked it around a bit by my sinful ways so my armor (along with the Holy Spirit) would not try to serve its purpose. As I was adhering to my flesh and when this happened, I was only satisfying what my flesh desired and was not living like I should have (see Romans 8:8). It is important to know that although I went to church, I was not pleasing God, even though I had on my Sunday's best. My best meant I did not have on God's best. I was not armored up, which left me subject to battle ill-prepared. Lack of armor created a big difference in how I looked to God and how I thought I looked to Him. Therefore, I had to set into action changes so that my life could represent an heir of His kingdom instead of representing Satan. As believers, we are to serve our purpose by denying our flesh and listening to the Holy Spirit so that we can be taught what our Father is wanting to teach us, and the best way to do this is to put on the full armor of God.

Keep faith and hope in God at all times. We keep the faith by loving our Father. Love Him by spending time with Him. Know that He is a forgiving God who loves you dearly. Guard every thought that comes to contradict your Father's love for you. Keep every piece of armor in position to protect you against the spirits and principalities of evil. Allowing spirits and principalities to have their way at our thoughts allows them to have access to removing our helmet of salvation. Our salvation reassures us that we are delivered from our sins.

If you think about it, nearly every attack that Satan thrusts at us is in our mind. He wants us to think less of ourselves. He wants us to feel condemned when our Father says we are forgiven. Satan wants us to become overwhelmed with depression, anxiety, and suicidal thoughts. He does this by getting us to chunk our helmet of salvation to the curb. He knows how it feels to be unforgiven by God because he is not forgiven, so he inflicts upon us what he feels. Satan is rejected by God.

Every thought he gives us is his very own thought of how he feels. They are not thoughts that we should be burdened with, but Satan knows how sin can appear as unforgivable and he uses his personal hurt from God against us. The closer you get to your Father and the closer you get to your purpose, the more Satan wants to battle with you.

Consider Judas, one of Jesus' disciples who walked with the Savior. He did not understand that even though Jesus knew of his wrongdoing prior to it being committed and knew what would happen to Him, forgiveness was available to him. Judas struggled to see that his Father still loved him despite his actions. He did not accept the love of Jesus as our forgiven Savior because his mind was plagued with Satan's continuous unworthy thoughts. The struggle to see God's love for us leaves us vulnerable to attacks. We often get earthly love confused with how our Father's unconditional love operates.

True love has been distorted by our earthly perception of love. Jesus' love is not the love that we experience on earth, where a person says they love you but does harm to you the moment you have opposite opinions. At no point did Jesus treat Judas indifferently. Therefore, when people seek to do you harm, understand that this is a test for you to allow the Holy Spirit to minister to you in love so that you will know what to do (see James

1:3-4). Your natural response would be to snatch off your armor and seek vengeance. However, vengeance is not yours to give (see Romans 12:19). When we unlawfully set out to get revenge on others for their mistreatment of us, we set in motion consequences that will delay others from seeing the kingdom of God in us. Yes, we have rights within the law, but when we engage in this manner, we should do it without bitterness or strife in our hearts. When we engage in earthly laws, we are to always be mindful of God's laws. If there is a conflict between earthly laws and God's, choose God's laws every time. The outcome will be far better.

In considering God's law, we begin to understand the power of our actions. We have the responsibility to follow the commandments with the Holy Spirit guiding and correcting us. Rarely do we speak of the commandments and follow them. We speak more so on the benefits of receiving from God without consideration of our responsibilities. We are to obey two very important commandments: to honor God as the one and only almighty God and to love our neighbor as ourselves (see Matthew 22:36-40). Accepting and living by these two commandments will result in a test. I know God will test me, and He will test you too. It is written in His Word. The test is coming, and how we respond during the test impacts the outcome (see James 1:3-4). Get excited when you endure the test knowing that this is part of God helping you to see who He is in your life. This is God showing you how you need to grow to be more like Him. This is God saying, "I am demonstrating my love through you for others to see." So, walk in love, because your Father is helping you to see how He works in your life. He is changing things so that you can now move knowing that there is only one God. He is almighty and powerful. Trust Him to intervene in every situation and know that He is able to help you through all things. Trusting Him will grow your faith. For this reason, we must keep our armor on so that we can be victorious.

You must realize that there is a continuous venomous attack to get us to discard our armor. Disposing our armor causes us to engage in battle unprepared, resulting in us being unable to enjoy victory with our heavenly Father as our Lord. Consider a soldier who has set out on his own and left camp to fight a battle without his weaponry. This action can lead to detrimental outcomes. Even when David went out to defeat the giant Goliath, he knew the power of his weaponry that was with him. He refused to put on the king's armor because he had not won a battle in the garb. He knew that his Father had been with him in battle before when he defeated wild animals that could have easily destroyed him. Instead of latching on to what others were saying, David kept his faith and was victorious. David knew the problem: that his family, the kingdom, and he himself faced death if he were to go into battle unprepared.

Unfortunately, that is how we have lived. Living life without our armor causes us not to consider our lives and the lives of others. Although we think we are doing the right thing, when we set out on our own without listening to our God, we allow ourselves to be surrounded by the enemy. For this reason, we start out by doing things our way. Then, we get into the middle of a situation and we realize that we are not prepared and not protected. We discern that there is no support group because we did not verify with God how we should have moved forward. We did not look at our situation and then look in the Bible to see what the Holy Spirit said we should do. We go out without God leading us only to retreat to Him to recover from our wounds. Sometimes, recovering from our wounds takes longer than we expected or anticipated, but had we trusted on God initially by consulting Him first before advancing forward, we would have been warned of the dangers that lay ahead. The most important thing is that we revert back to God. We do this knowing that He loves us, and He is so glad to see us coming back to Him. Let me tell you I have done this several times. Even now as I walk with Jesus and seek God's advice, I still get caught skipping off on a path, but I hear God say come back a lot faster than I did in the past, so I quickly retreat.

In my actions, God reminds me daily to not be anxious (see Philippians 4:6). I love it when I am making decisions and the other person requests that I hurry up and get in on the deal. No, I am not moving forward or advancing, because this situation has not been given to me as a clearance to move onward. Although God has given us ideas, we need to know when it is time to move forward, when it is time to listen, and when it is time to disengage. No war is won when soldiers are doing their own thing. As believers who do their own thing, we become prey who will later regret decisions.

It has been very important for me to know what the Bible says about a situation so that I can stop acting like the world. Remember, we are peculiar people who do not have to fight battles like others (see 1 Peter 2:9). We have the presence of the Holy Spirit in us, so that gives us an advantage. Listening to Him to know what He directs us to do gives us godly insight. The ability to hear the Holy Spirit is made easier when we have on the full armor of God. Trust me, if I had put my armor on, I would not have made the errors I made because I was people-pleasing, did not know my purpose, sought to make the lives of others more comfortable, and wanted to be a part of a group that was not part of the kingdom. The damages I encountered wounded me mentally, financially, and physically, yet I thrive today because of God who loves me.

Our wounds are not designed for us to feel bad about who we are and what we have done. Our wounds give us a chance to say, "I was wounded in battle because I did not have my armor on, which allowed the enemy to attack me." However, I am under the rulership of my Lord who loves me, and He is guiding me to healing. It is incredible once you understand this principle. Go to God, not just on Sunday. The Bible says we should pray, read the Bible, fast, and serve others as part of our daily lives (see 2 Chronicles 7:14). We are required to behave not like the world with an "eye for an eye" or a "tooth for a tooth" mentality, physically, or spiritually. We are required to follow in the ways of God and do His will. If there is a need to take legal action against someone, you have the right to do it. However, ask God to give you direction on how you should proceed. He will speak to you through the Holy Spirit. Trust God's plan even though you do not understand it.

Grab Your Armor!

Go grab your armor – the war is on. Your armor provides protection. It replaces what we wore because we were born in sin. In other words, we need to put armor on because when we are born, we have on the world's armor, which is derived from selfish desires that lead to us not doing what our loving Father asks. As a result, we end up doing the opposite of what He instructed. When we consider our armor that our Lord provides and what the opposite of it is and what our natural response would be to a situation, we see the importance of why our Father gave us this gift. Because of this danger, we are commanded to put on the full armor – not just parts of it when we think we should. We have to keep on the entire armor at all times and never take it off.

The whole armor is our gift of love from our caring Father. If you doubt that your Father loves you, consider why Jesus was sent. He was sent because of God's love (see John 3:16). He loves us and cares about our life now and our life as immortal spirits. Accepting that you are loved by your Father impacts your faith. Remember, we can only have faith because we love our Father. His love gift to us covers every area of our lives so that we can live in His presence and be seen by Him as one who loves Him. To exemplify our love for Him, we must keep the faith and obey His commandments, which are based on love.

The Belt of Truth

A belt in the physical realm keeps clothing from falling off us, which would result in being improperly exposed. Therefore, a belt of truth will also keep us from being exposed as one who is not obedient. Jesus says whatever is done in the dark will be brought into the light (see Mark 12:2-3). In other words, do not try to justify and hide what is not true, because your pants will come down and you will be exposed. Maybe you are thinking that you have done a lot of things and have gotten away with it. Regardless of who knows on earth, God knows, and unless you are one who believes in Jesus' resurrection and striving to obey the commandments under the guidance of the Holy Spirit, you will not fall under grace, but under judgment (see Romans 6). You will be judged, and your secret lies will come to be known at the most challenging time by the only one who could have saved you (see Romans 8:12-13).

Remember, we are forgiven when we sin by breaking the commandments, but the difference is as believers, we are seen as the righteousness of God because we believe Jesus is our Savior, and we are allowing the Holy Spirit to keep the will of God conscious in our lives (see Romans 8:1-4). We are not trying to get to heaven by merely following the commandments, because simply trying to follow the commandments without accepting Jesus as our savior places us under condemnation. Our belief in Jesus positions us under grace instead of condemnation. However, we must be mindful that grace does not give us authorization to run amok like a sinner who has no God, but it protects us as we live life under the direction of the Holy Spirit.

Therefore, be truthful in every manner and in every way. Do not seek to deceive others by saying one thing that is partly true when in reality, you have been commanded to be completely truthful. When you are presented with opportunities to lie so that you can look better, do *not* do it! This deception will be revealed at some point. Stop. Do not engage. Walk in the truth of knowing who you are and believe that God has provided you with what you need to be a conqueror. Armor up in truth. God will make a way. If you lie about things, then it is as if you are saying, "I am taking this into my own hands." Better yet, since Satan is the Father of lies, you are serving the prince of darkness (see John 8: 43-44).

Being truthful is very important. Do not let others try to convince you to believe that what they say, or their way of deception is hidden from God. Know that as believers, some of us are on different levels, and when others present you with an untruthful way of dealing with a situation, see it as an opportunity to show God some love. Do not engage to boost your reputation. Do not engage in lying to cover up or to make yourself seem great, as this will lead to lies that can be uncovered. For this reason, God reminds us that all liars will be thrown into the lake of fire, as we are not acting like God, but like Satan (see Revelation 21:8). Satan is the father of lies, and through his lies, he even got Eve to disobey her Heavenly Father, whom she had a personal relationship with. Flee from lying. Go quick and grab your belt before you are exposed. No one wants the world to see the things that should not be seen, especially during the day of judgment. Notice this is the first part of the armor that we are commanded to put on, which signifies its importance, because Jesus is the way, the truth, and the life (see John 14:6). We cannot even get to our Father without the truth – without Jesus. Lies block us from being heard, as we have the Holy Spirit in us and His presence in us allows us to have God within us. God is not a liar, so we should not lie (Numbers 23:19). Lying only deceives some people, and sometimes it is a momentary deception.

The Holy Spirit knows our heart and goes to our Father to tell Him the truth about who we really are. He is also our advocate that presents our case on our behalf. I would rather have Him be my advocate speaking on my behalf than for me to represent myself. The Holy Spirit also speaks to us so we can know how we should live. Listening to Him strengthens us and prevents us from being condemned by Satan. What is the Holy Spirit revealing to you about changes you should make or how to move forward in your relationship with others? Without receiving the truth from the Holy Spirit, we lose connection to our Lord. Apparently, living a life of lies does not lead to Jesus being on the mainline. Instead, it leads to Satan instigating. We will get a "busy" signal from our Father when we manipulate lies, so it is very integral for us to grab the belt of truth and disconnect from the father of lies.

If I had my belt of truth, I would not have lied, orchestrated situations, and misused men for my own pleasure. My belt was nowhere to be found. I needed to change from my manipulative ways so I could be well prepared for the battle. The spiritual forces of evil are out to dismantle everything we believe is true. We are in battle with these spiritual forces of evil that have set up as host in our bodies as if they own us. In their way of making things appear as if they are our choice, they present things that are pleasing to our flesh (see Luke 11:26). Therefore, receive and wear the belt of truth, knowing its value. Being truthful allows us to have open communication with our Father through the Holy Spirit and it prevents us from enduring the second death, because all liars are going to hell (see Revelation 21:8). Stop sinning and ask for forgiveness. Even if you do sin, always know that you are forgiven as soon as you ask for forgiveness. Allow God to guide you daily by placing your belt of truth around your waist so that your exposure will not result in the embarrassment of not having your name written in the book of life, because on that day, it will be too late.

The Breastplate of Righteousness

Are we living a righteous life, or are we taking advantage of the concept of being righteous? To be seen as righteous indicates that we believe that God raised

Jesus our Lord from the dead and that we believe that Jesus was sent from our Father to earth (see Romans 4:20-25). Because of this belief, we are no longer judged by the law as being righteous (see Romans 10:4). We have been redeemed by Jesus. Don't you like it when you receive something good automatically?

I recall the other day when I went to the pet store to get dog food after learning that Mocha, one of my dogs, had food allergies. There is a certain type of food that she has to get, and I noticed there were several brands. As I walked around, I began to place different brands in my basket because I wasn't sure which brand would be best. As I was turning the corner, I noticed a brand on the endcap that was listed as one of the better brands to get for dogs with food allergies. As I looked at the big bag, I noticed that it was on sale for twenty dollars less than the regular price. I grabbed two twelve-pound bags and walked to the front of the store. Because I wasn't sure if both the salmon and the chicken were on sale, I asked for a price check. You cannot imagine how I felt when she said it was $19.99. That's right, a $46.99 bag of food was now more than half off. Thank You, Father, for the godly discount. You see, everyone loves it when they get something good without a hassle. That's righteousness. That's also how favor works too. Thank You, Father, for Your favor.

Similarly, righteousness is given to all believers through faith in Jesus (see Romans 3:22). Abraham believed in God. This made him righteous (see Genesis 15:6). However, as believers who were born under the new covenant, we are righteous because we believe in God's ability to raise Jesus from the dead. Accepting that Jesus died for our sins and was raised from the dead means Jesus was victorious over death for our sins and was raised to life for our justification. Therefore, because of Jesus, we are redeemed from sin and God does not see us as sinful. We are justified or seen as being virtuous, not as losers, sinners, or ungodly people. Our sins are hidden because of our belief. We are the righteousness of God – meaning we are God's excellent children (see 2 Corinthians 5:21). Isn't that amazing?

Notice where the breastplate is located. It covers our chest and protects our vital organs. It is a covering that protects the body parts we need in order for us to survive. In other words, in order for us to exist as immortal beings, our most vital part is covered with righteousness, allowing us to be seen by God as His virtuous children. We obtain this gift of righteousness because of our willingness to believe that Jesus is able to redeem us by His actions on earth, which included walking on earth, not sinning, dying on the cross, suffering separation from God, and trusting God at His word to raise Him from the dead. Jesus endured everything for us and He set an example of how we should live as believers. Like Jesus trusted that God would raise Him from the dead, we must also trust Him in our daily actions. With the presence of the Holy Spirit in us, God helps us overcome all obstacles and every challenge we encounter. We must totally release the situation to Him and believe in His ability to do what our mind tells us is impossible but our spirit reassures us is possible. As a result, we will live and be welcomed into the kingdom of Heaven.

Realize that righteousness is our weapon (see 2 Corinthians 6:7). It is a weapon because when the spirits of darkness try to tell you that you are unworthy because of your past, when Satan tells you that you deserved what you got, or when Satan speaks harshly to you to the point that you feel bad about yourself, remember the truth about how virtuous you are in God's sight. God does not see you as anything other than a virtuous, upright person who has the gift within them to fulfill His purpose. Always remember that Satan is a liar and that is what he does all the time. He uses people to impose these negative thoughts into your mind, or he might present them in your thoughts because of the emotional struggle that you are going through. Please know that all his words are nonsense. He is just babbling because he is out to destroy you with his wild comments and words of discouragement (see 1 Peter 5:8-11).

When you recognize these lies portrayed to you in your thoughts, pay attention, and connect these thoughts with who is putting them into your mind. Know that Satan is trying to mutilate you, but if you resist him by keeping the faith in God, he will flee. Be strong in the Lord's way of doing things and know in your heart that you are not the only one who is being faced with the same battle. Endure the struggle and stay encouraged. Replace every lie that Satan tells you with, "God loves me." Replace every feeling he tries to impose on you knowing that's exactly how Satan feels. He wants to manipulate you with his feelings of rejection. When you resist him, he will flee (see James 4:7). Endure this suffering for a little while and keep the faith so that God will use His power to restore you (see Psalm 30:5). He will make you strong, firm, and steadfast.

In order to be seen as righteous, we need to believe and be baptized to fulfill the covenant of righteousness (see Matthew 3:15). Our righteousness through Christ surpasses that of the pharisees and the teacher of the law, as they use laws to be little others and keep them from growing in Christ (see Matthew 5:20). Their ways of living and doing things were not so that God could get the glory, they were so they could be seen as greater than the one who committed the sin. Therefore, as believers, we must be dead to sin and to the concept of ridicule. Those who ridicule you are doing their job, but will you? We are to remain faithful and become dead to sin. By being dead to sin and not allowing our lives to reflect sinful behaviors, we become established on purpose. Each day we strive to become dead to sin by listening to the Holy Spirit. Even in the midst of sinning, the Holy Spirit will speak to you. Listen for His voice, repent, and live forgiven. We cannot work to achieve righteousness. Righteousness is a gift to us as believers in Jesus (see Romans 5:17). We represent the righteous and we are not judged by the law (see Romans 7:6). So, when you take off your shield of righteousness and live as you choose, you are putting yourself in a path that can result in judgment as one who is unrighteous. Although it might appear challenging to walk as God directs, remember that His yoke is easy and His burdens are light (see Matthew 11:29-30). Our Father will teach us how to walk and have peace in Him through the Holy Spirit.

As righteous people, we should automatically implement the "love walk". Sure, there will be moments when we may think, *Um, I don't think so*, but the Holy Spirit will guide us so that we will know what to do. Our walk with our Father will direct us. In contrast, engaging in sinful acts simply because we know we are saved by grace is rebellious sinful behavior. Sure, we may stumble, but we are not to continue to act like sinners. When we recognize our ways as not being godly, repenting leads to forgiveness every time. Don't get stuck in your sin like I was. There are far greater things that your Father has for you. These distractions from Satan are his way of keeping us with a peasant mentality when God sees us as His heirs.

As I read Romans, I started to think, *Well, maybe we cannot appear unrighteous to God,* so I prayed for insight. During the night, I was guided by the Holy Spirit to read and reflect on these scriptures for clarification. Jesus said that during the day of judgement, there will be many who will come to Him and say that they casted out demons in His name, and Jesus will say, "I never knew you" (see Matthew 7:21-23). Although they were aware of the power of God in them, these believers' sinful ways apparently contradicted what they believed. I make this assumption about their behavior for two reasons. First, those who live sinful and contrary to God will be cast into the lake of fire (Revelation 21:8). Secondly, these individuals must have believed that with the Holy Spirit, they could heal and cast out demons. Consider this: when Jesus was identified as being able to cast out demons because He was under Beelzebub, the prince of demons (see Matthew 12:24)? When they made this inaccurate assumption, Jesus quickly informed them that a kingdom divided cannot stand, and to say that one casting out demons is not by the Spirit of God is blasphemy (see Matthew 12:25-32). Therefore, we should be very mindful in thinking that because we have the gifts of the Spirit, we cannot go to hell. We cannot intentionally sin without asking for forgiveness and allowing the Holy Spirit to instruct us. It is important to act when the Holy Spirit speaks to us about our behavior. We should not ignore Him or discredit His presence or power (see 1 Thessalonians 5:19).

With this in mind, we have to actively be doing the will of God instead of opting to keep sinning. God's grace is not like an unlimited credit account in which you never have to pay. His grace is sufficient to all, but we have a responsibility. We are to operate as representatives of the kingdom of God.

Because we are seen through the redemption of Jesus as the righteous people of God, we are to keep the royal law – that is, we are to love our neighbor as if they were a part of us (see James 2:8). In other words, we should be very careful in how we treat everyone we encounter; this also includes social media communication. Showing love, being compassionate, and exemplifying mercy allows us to walk in harmony with each other. Therefore, live knowing that you represent our Lord and that your actions should replicate the life of an heir who has inherited righteousness. Live knowing who you are: the righteous heir.

Feet in Peace

Our feet are to be covered in the gospel of peace, meaning our feet should be in the good news, which allows us to walk in the gospel of peace. What is the good news? The good news is the kingdom of God (see Mark 1:14, Luke 4:43), and the only way that we have peace is through Jesus (see Isaiah 53:5). Our Lord's peace allows us to be in some of the most challenging situations without losing our cool. His peace will guard our soul, which is our heart and minds (see Philippians 4:7). The Holy Spirit will guide us to walk in peace so that our actions lead to bringing others to Christ.

We cannot walk in peace without the Holy Spirit's intervention. Without the Holy Spirit, we struggle to control our responses and reactions to situations. We want to do things our way so that we can be the one making the decisions, but when we learn that we are not our own and we are God's, it will help us connect to the Holy Spirit. Allowing Him to work in us keeps us at peace with others. When in a challenging situation that tries to take your peace, consider that Jesus was chastised for us to have peace (see Isaiah 53:5). Remembering Jesus helps us endure. Walking in peace shows that we trust the Holy Spirit and seek His input for guidance. Peacemakers who sow in peace reap a harvest of righteousness (see James 3:18) As the righteous children of God, we speak with wisdom and what is just (see Psalm 37:29). Hence, being peaceful in situations by controlling what we let fly out of our mouths is wise. Therefore, seek peace – your future awaits you (see Psalm 37:36-37).

The Shield of Faith

Have you got your shield up? The shield of faith puts out all the fires that the evil one and his partners try to throw at us (see Ephesians 6:16). Satan always has a thought to project at us, especially when we are following what God says. We need our shield to overcome all the obstacles we encounter in life. Notice that all he can do is send flaming arrows, but our faith is our defender against anything he sends our way. Faith is confirmed when we receive the things we hoped for prior to their existence (see Hebrews 11:1). Because we are fighting the good fight of faith, victory is already ours even before Satan sends one arrow of negativity our way. Therefore, keeping faith in what God says defeats Satan every time. He can only try to tell us lies to create doubt in our minds.

Each one of us is given faith, but how much depends on our mindset. Although we have the mind of the Lord, Satan tries to pollute our mind (see 1 Corinthians 2:16). That is a powerful statement that we need to embrace. You and I have the mind of the Lord. Our mind becomes transformed to think like God when we keep the faith while working on our relationship with Him. Each one of us has been given a specific amount or measure of faith (see Romans 12:3). How we operate in faith influences how our faith grows. It is like the parable that Jesus told about the talents. Each servant was given a certain number of talents (see Matthew 25:14-30). Those servants who used their talent increased the amount they had, but the one who hid his talent saw no increase. These talents are like faith. Each one of us have been given a measure of faith to believe in God to make a way for us. What we do with our faith makes our Father happy. As we operate in faith by keeping hope in God's intervention in our lives, our faith grows. We continue to believe in our Father's love for us because He will demonstrate it by continuously showing up in our lives to make things happen for us. He will continuously protect us and show up when we trust Him to come forth in our lives.

Understanding that our faith continues to grow as we trust in our Father to be there for us is the mindset that we should have. Our carnal mind that thinks like this world separates us from being dependent on our loving Father. That is why we are urged not to think like the world. Instead, transforming our minds to think like God should be part of our daily life (see Romans 12:2). Notice that we must transform our mind. God does not do this. We must control our thoughts and direct them to think like God wants us to think. At times, this might seem like a challenge, but when we call on our Father to help us, He will. He will give you strength to see another day. He will open doors for you so you can just walk right in. Your Father will allow things to look hopeless because He wants us to totally trust in Him and to see Him intervening in our lives.

Consider Jehoshaphat. He was warned that a vast army was coming to destroy him. What he did next is an example of what we should do. He prayed. He did not give a prayer of worry, but one of trust. His prayer signifies to us how to operate in faith. We are not to look at the situation, but we are to go to our almighty God and have faith in His strength. Our willingness to submit to Him and keep the faith in Him demonstrates our love and trust in God. That is why it is imperative that we transform our minds to think like our Lord with the guidance of the Holy Spirit. Thinking like our Lord automatically sends our every concern directly to Him. Having our Lord's mindset transfers every praise directly to our God. When He intervenes in our lives, we know immediately that it was Him, and we give Him the credit for saving us. Having the mind of our Lord allows us to have the desires of our heart because our mind thinks like Him. Thinking like our Father allows us to be able to talk to Him about how we would like things to transpire and have the outcome even better than what we discussed with Him. The outcome in every situation is all based on our faith in our Father's ability to do what He says He will do and loving Him enough not to doubt His will to do good in our lives.

When we have faith in God, we do not have to worry about what we shall eat or what we will wear because He knows what we need and He provides these things to us (see Matthew 6:34). Unfortunately, many of our thoughts are based on our needs, and when Satan feeds us doubt, we allow our peace to flee. Worrying about earthly issues causes us to be afflicted with anxiety, frustration, and depression. Remember, Satan is a great deliverer of these feelings because he feels this way. He has internalized these feelings because he is no longer connected to the love of God. Because he knows how it really feels to be rejected by God, he projects these feelings onto us. This is a very important point that I want you to understand. Satan knows his end will be hell. There is no hope for him, so projecting thoughts of hopelessness in us and feelings of disconnection from our Father is what he desires. He wants us to distrust our Father so that he won't be alone in hell. I'm sure you have met people with this same mindset. If they are miserable, they want you to feel the same way. That behavior is ungodly and comes from Satan. The desire to pull you and I down with him is one of the most selfish ways that Satan has. His meticulous plan to defeat us by conforming our minds to the bondage of doubt allows lack, need, depression, anxiety along with other degrading feelings to continuously plague our minds. However, by not worrying about things that we have been commanded by God not to worry about, we increase our faith in our Father. When worry and doubt seeps in, remember that our Father is standing right there to protect us.

This reminds me of one of my favorite scenes in The Lion King. Remember when Simba went to the elephant graveyard with Nala? The hyenas had been scheming and waiting for this moment. They cornered Nala and Simba with the hopes of annihilating them. Right when things looked extremely deadly for the young lion cubs, Mufasa stepped in to rescue them. That's how I see my Father rescuing me when I am in situations where I do not know what to do. Walking by faith and not by sight means that we keep planting seeds in the crop and God will produce good fruit for us. As we walk in faith by doing what God has directed us to do, it appears challenging at times because we do not see the end results, but we must keep the faith.

Our love for our Father encourages us to keep working and trusting Him despite how the situation appears. Staying encouraged and knowing that we will benefit from the harvest we planted requires faith. As we go through life, God will direct us to plant all our seeds in healthy soil. In other words, our Father will tell us who to trust when making decisions, where to tithe, and how to invest our time. There is great danger in planting in bad soil for selfish reasons or ill-gain. That is why we must seek the counsel of the Holy Spirit daily to know what God is directing us to do. We only need faith as small as a mustard seed to be victorious. Plant your seed of faith in your loving Father and believe Him to reign in every situation. Stay encouraged by reading the Bible, praying, and worshiping Him.

Did you notice how faith is the only weapon that can increase or decrease based on our trust in our Father? Our mind has to constantly be set to think on what God says. For this reason, meditating on the Word of God assures us that our Father will work things out. While meditating on the Word, the Holy Spirit allows me to see a key point that I had overlooked. As I mediate, I see a message from my Father to me. Quickly, I record this love message from my Father, and I read it over and over again until it is affirmed in my mind. Writing these out as affirmations and saying them empowers my faith. There have even been dreams that I have had, and when I feel disheartened because they do not appear to be transpiring, I visualize the dream and internalize the feeling of living life as I saw it in my dream. I recall how I was dressed, the conversations that I heard, and where I was. Visualizing helps me see what my Father has promised me and it encourages me to keep going while believing in Him. That is why it is important to awaken in the morning armored up with the shield of faith. I intentionally live like this because it allows God to fulfill his purpose in my existence, which is grounded in showing the world His power through us (see 1 Peter 4:10). So, I want to encourage you to keep your faith in God. Allow the Holy Spirit to operate in your life and find strength in knowing that faith is a gift that has unimaginable power.

The Helmet of Salvation

Guarding our mind is integral because our mind impacts our entire existence. For this reason, we are to put on our helmet of salvation. Why is a salvation seen as a helmet? When we consider the importance of the helmet in protecting our mind and our brain, we realize its vitality. Surely we have heard how people have been brain dead but still have other functions of their body operating, yet they are declared dead. This illustration is how we operate when our mind is not shielded with salvation. It is if we are living in this world, but we are not operating as Christians should. We are spiritually dead. We appear to be alive in Christ, but our actions, our faith, and our thoughts are not in harmony with God. For this reason, having the helmet of salvation makes things clear in our mind regarding how to operate in faith because we know that we have been rescued from sin.

The helmet of salvation protects our mind and re-assures us that we have been delivered from sin by Jesus. Salvation guards our thoughts when the enemy comes to attack us. If you notice, when he comes, he always has something negative to say or he is always trying to get us to do things opposite of what God says. Being mindful of his tricks to get us to operate without salvation gives us the upper hand. We know that Satan always wants us to think less of ourselves. He always wants us to feel unloved by our Father through condemnation. However, when we embrace the truth that no matter what we encounter, our God will save and protect us, we dismantle Satan's agenda. Believing that Jesus is our salvation (see Psalm 62) and that we are loved guards our mind from the enemy. Therefore, we should not become overwhelmed with the stresses of life, because no matter what happens, God is our salvation, which makes him our refuge when we encounter troubling times or situations. We are to trust our Lord and know that what He said in His Word is true. God has given us grace so that we can enjoy the blessing of salvation. He will rescue us (see Titus 2:11). Keeping on our helmet of salvation, trusting in God always, and finding comfort in knowing that He is our protector will always give us peace.

As we keep on our helmet of salvation, our thoughts should be based on biblical principles in which our God interacts on our behalf in every turn. Nothing presented to us should cause us to change our thinking and believe anything besides what our Lord promised us. He has our back. This is evident when we read every passage in the Bible. He is with us, and He will protect us. We might not see how we can make it out of a situation, and we might not see how we will overcome it, but we have to remember that our almighty God impacts the spiritual world to create manifestations in the physical world. In other words, we might not see how things are changing, but as long as you count on God to solve your problems and not yourself, you will overcome and be victorious.

To have this victory controlling our thoughts is crucial. Therefore, during the season of trials and temptations, we have to be like Job and think like him even when it appears as if we are losing and feel like we are being defeated, we have to keep on believing in God (see Job 13:7) and count it as a joyous moment because God thought enough of us to test us (see James 1:2). When we move from our selfish way of thinking about trials and see the beauty of the test as an opportunity to witness to others about how God brought us out of the storm, it influences our journey. When on the journey, what we repeatedly say in our mind influences the impact that the spiritual forces of darkness have on us. Therefore, we should always have scriptures on our mind when we are attacked with thoughts of discontent. Remember when Michael was dealing with Satan? He spoke with authority when he said, "The Lord rebukes you" (see Jude 1:9). We have the right to say the same thing when we are bombarded with thoughts of self-hate. That's how we must think of self-hate from the enemy, because any time he wants us to go against our Father, he is asking us to hate ourselves because our Father is our creator.

Have you ever noticed that when we *do* go against our Father, Satan is the first one to ridicule us with thoughts of disobedience? He plays both sides so that we can always feel conflicted. However, knowing that our Father loves us and that He forgives us helps us to keep going in love. Don't ever allow Satan to present his illusions as truth anymore. They are lies nestled in his feelings of separation from our Father. So, keep calling on our Father to work things out for you. The liar will flee because he has no power over us. He can only instigate to create confusion. Grab your helmet of salvation and know that nothing can remove it. It's still part of your armor even if you sin, because asking for forgiveness places everything back into alignment with God. Therefore, repent, know that you are forgiven, and strut around with your helmet of salvation.

The Sword

For years, my sword was only dragged to church on Sundays. It was never used for anything except for scripture readings during the sermon. At home, when I tried to read the Bible, immediately, I would fall asleep as if I had taken a sleeping pill. However, this is now my favorite piece of equipment because it helps me to understand the power I have with my other artillery. Without my Bible, I was powerless and exposed, living a life with no regard as to how my behavior impacted others. I cared less about my brother and more about myself. Yes, I had a Bible during those years of deception and selfish gain, but I never spent time reading it. I never sat down to get an in-depth understanding of God's truth. Therefore, without reading my Bible for understanding, I was rendered a soldier in battle with equipment for which I had not read the manual on how to use, nor had I sought my commanding officer for instruction. Without spending time reading the Bible daily to gain understanding, the only knowledge about my tools that I received was on Sundays. During each service, the minister provided information, but if it was not for the equipment I needed for a certain battle, I was ill prepared. For this reason, we are to study to show ourselves approved so that we can understand who the Father is and how to live focused on Him (see

2 Timothy 2:15). Reading the Word helps us prepare for battle.

As we read, knowing that every word was approved by God and was only written because He authorized it helps us internalize how powerful each scripture is (see 2 Timothy 3:16-17). When I began reading, I started out reading the same scriptures daily. As I continued, my scripture time changed to reading books of the Bible. Now, God directs me to passages that He uses to speak directly to my situation. Each scripture reflects love and faith in Him. They encourage and comfort me so that I am able to make it through the day knowing that my Father speaks to me to reassure me that everything is going to be alright. Surely this explains why the Word is a lamp unto my feet, as the Word directs me and luminates the path so I can walk in faith (see Psalm 119:105). Jesus even used the scriptures to flick Satan away (see Matthew 4:4). Since we have the mind of Christ, we can implement the same principles that He did to get the same results. Jesus said that we can do greater things because of the Holy Spirit in us (see John 14:12). It is time to do greater works, and the only way we can do great things is by becoming familiar with how to live life by faith under the guidance of the Holy Spirit.

Now, I understand the impact that reading my Bible daily has on my life. I have seen how it has helped me tremendously. Reading guides me to see life differently, or shall I say it advises me to see things spiritually. Because the words in the Bible are sharper than a two-edged sword, it has helped me acknowledge areas that need rectifying. It is so sharp until it can divide between our soul and our spirit (see Hebrews 4:12 - 14). The Word of God's ability to divide two invisible things allows us to see how it is able to penetrate our every thought to help us see the truth regarding God's ways. Reading daily keeps our inner thoughts in alignment with God so that we can follow Him. Live daily, ready for battle with your sword in position for combat instead of in the backseat of your car.

Pray in the Spirit

Our final weapon that we have is often overlooked, and that is praying in the Spirit which is praying in tongues. Praying in tongues is our mic-drop! There is no need to worry about anything when we pray in the Spirit because what we pray goes directly to our Father (see 1 Corinthians 14:12). If you have the gift of praying in the Spirit, praying daily is powerful. Your message goes straight to our Father and He understands every word.

Perhaps you are thinking, *I don't speak in tongues.* If you do not speak in tongues, don't worry! God has you covered, because the Holy Spirit knows your heart and He goes to the Father on your behalf as your advocate.

So, do not become concerned, because God has made a way for all of us to be able to get our message to Him. Therefore, pray continuously (see 1 Thessalonians 5:16-18), and if you want the gift of speaking in tongues, ask God. He will grant you the desires of your heart.

If you do not pray in the Spirit, please say the following prayer and believe that you will receive the gift of speaking in tongues:

My Father, I trust You with all things in my life. I openly confess my belief in You. Every word written in the Bible is true. My soul and spirit embrace these truths. Your Word says that whatever we ask for, You will provide. I believe in the gift of speaking in tongues and I ask You to grant me this gift to me today. Father, give me this gift so that I can pray in your godly language directly to You when I need You to hear my true cry and praise. I love You, Father, and I trust Your word. As I speak in utterance, I will forever worship you. In Jesus' name, I pray and believe that I have the gift of speaking in tongues. Amen.

Now, open your mouth and allow the words to flow out without allowing your mind to take control. Know that everything is possible for the one who believes (see Mark 9:23). Keep prompting God and believing until speaking in tongues is manifested in your life. I also suggest that we pray and acknowledge the Holy Spirit. This prayer helps to remind us of the God in us and it makes us more aware of His presence. Can you imagine living in a house with someone that you never speak to? That is exactly how we behave when we ignore the Holy Spirit. For many years, I blocked multiple messages the Holy Spirit tried to tell me. He was speaking, and I was like, "Whatever." That was so horrible of me to behave in such a way. Let's be real, when a person does not greet us, we wonder what is wrong with them. For this reason, I pray daily, speak to the Holy Spirit, and sit quietly. This quiet time after prayer allows me to hear from my Father. Please say the following prayer:

Dear Father, thank You for the new covenant. Your covenant of love gives me access to the kingdom of God. It allows You to be in the hearts and minds of Your children. Gladly, I welcome the Holy Spirit into my mind and my heart. With His active presence in my life, I ask Him to provide direction, guidance, and protection so that I will make good decisions based on biblical principles. I know that insight from the Holy Spirit is instruction from You, Father, and I am grateful for Your presence in every decision I make today. In Jesus' name I pray, amen.

After saying this prayer, sit quietly for fourteen minutes. Listen for Him to speak to you. Make this part of your daily life requirements so that you can learn to hear the Holy Spirit's voice when He speaks to you.

As part of my prayer life, I have been commanded to say the Lord's Prayer at least three times a day. I even say it before eating. Intentionally, God has given me this requirement because as I am walking in faith, there are moments when my mind wants to say in prayer things that do not align with what God says. For this reason, I know my prayers would be complaints about a situation that God is well aware of. Therefore, saying the Lord's Prayer helps me speak to my almighty Father and provides an opportunity for me to pray as Jesus says I should. It is a prayer of reverence and dependency on the one God who can save me. I trust Him to forever comfort and provide more than I can think or imagine. By praying the Lord's Prayer, my mind is reset to focus on Him as the only one I can depend on. Knowing that my Father loves me and provides for me discredits anything that the enemy wants me to believe because my Father rules on earth and in heaven. I trust His plan for my life and I am thirsty to know more of His righteousness so that I can be filled with faith. Faith in my Father confirms my love for Him and I will forever reverence His mighty name so that I can walk according to His will for my life.

Embrace this belief in God. He wants us to be victorious in every aspect of our lives. Victory in Him radiates beams of hope for the world that are brighter than the intense heat of the sun on the hottest day in the desert. Living victorious requires us to understand the power that we have with the presence of the Holy Spirit in us. Connecting to this power dismantles all things that come against us. Study God's Word to learn how caring and thoughtful He is. While learning of God's Word and finding out what is true, spending quality time reading the Bible and meditating on the Word is very influential on our understanding of what God is specifically saying to us. Doing these activities allows the Holy Spirit to speak to us and for us.

We are not powerless. We have an entire weaponry system to combat all that we encounter in life. These are all gifts from our Father, who knows how to defeat the enemy because He has already overpowered him. Get your armor and use it to live a triumphant life on earth. Without these gifts, we will struggle to enjoy the promises that God made to us, and we allow Satan to be the king of the hill. That is one ending to the story that is a lie. Satan does not have reign over our lives. Like dress up dolls, we have allowed Satan to exchange our WARdrobe for our Sunday's best. Stop playing dress-up. From this day forward, gather your WARdrobe essentials and armor up!

About the Author

Carla DeBro is an author, inventor, and investor who has experienced rejection not only from those around her, but also from her own inner thoughts. Living a lie of being happily entwined with lust and selfishness became her way of existence until she heard God's voice calling her to implement change. Accepting that she could no longer deny the presence of God in her life, she made drastic changes that left her battling rejection, financial struggles, and isolation. While dealing with these emotions, she found love, freedom, and purpose in God.

No longer bound by her past mistakes, she is now able to share how God sent her exactly what she needed in her life to help her overcome. He sent His love, and with His love, Carla was able to thrive. She made a WARdrobe change that left her feeling empowered, secure, and capable of completing the assignment that God gave her. Her assignment is to share how she no longer feels dejected because of her past. Because she no longer feels dejected, she can now share how she got caught up in sex, lies, and tragedies that lead to unhealthy decisions which plagued her life.

Boldly, she is admitting how unhealthy decisions along with guilt and shame limited her acceptance of God's love in her life. Now, she lives in His love without feeling the condemnation for her past. Her desire is for everyone to receive forgiveness without guilt and live the life God wants them to live by exploiting the devil instead of allowing him to exploit them.

Carla's message is for everyone to tell their truth and deny Satan's lies, because together, by walking in our healing, the glory of God will radiate around the world.

CPSIA information can be obtained
at www.ICGtesting.com
Printed in the USA
LVHW010619180621
690568LV00009B/706

9 781647 736163